Contents

OVERLEAF: A multiflash film exposure freezes the action of a green lacewing in three images: as it takes off vertically from a hawthorn leaf, throttles its flight by inverting its four fragile wings like an out-of-control umbrella and then comes in for a backward landing on the same leaf.

Wild, Wild World of Animals

Insects
& Spiders

A TIME-LIFE TELEVISION BOOK

Editor: Eleanor Graves
Series Editor: Charles Osborne
Text Editor: Richard Oulahan
  Associate Text Editor: Bonnie Johnson
  Author: John Neary
  Assistant Editor: Peter Ainslie
  Writer: Don Earnest
  Literary Research: Ellen Schachter
  Text Research: Gail Nussbaum
  Copy Editors: Robert J. Myer, Greg Weed
Picture Editor: Richard O. Pollard
  Picture Research: Judith Greene
  Permissions: Cecilia Waters
Book Designer and Art Director: Jos. Trautwein
  Art Assistant: Carl Van Brunt
Production Coordinator: Jane L. Quinson

WILD, WILD WORLD OF ANIMALS
TELEVISION PROGRAM
Producers: Jonathan Donald and Lothar Wolff
This Time-Life Television Book is published by Time-Life Films, Inc.
Bruce L. Paisner, *President*
J. Nicoll Durrie, *Vice President*

THE AUTHOR

JOHN NEARY was a reporter for the Washington *Star*, a writer for *Life* for 12 years and the author of two books, *Julian Bond: Black Rebel* and *Whom the Gods Destroy*. He has also written articles on conservation for many nature magazines.

THE CONSULTANTS

GERALD THOMPSON is the senior director of Oxford Scientific Films Ltd. in England, a company that specializes in the making of wildlife films. His background includes two decades as an entomologist in the Oxford University Department of Forestry, where he began a series of award-winning films.

JOHN COOKE is a director of Oxford Scientific Films Ltd. He is a world authority on spiders and their relatives and a specialist in biological still photography. Before joining O. S. F., Dr. Cooke lectured at Oxford University and was a member of the staff of the American Museum of Natural History in New York.

Wild, Wild World of Animals

Insects
& Spiders

Based on the television series
Wild, Wild World of Animals

Published by

TIME-LIFE FILMS

The excerpt from The Life of the Scorpion by J. Henri Fabre, translated by Alexander Teixeira de Mattos, is reprinted by permission of Dodd, Mead & Co., Inc. Copyright 1923 by Dodd, Mead & Co., Inc. Copyright renewed 1950 by Geoffrey William Russell. Acknowledgment to Hughes Massie Ltd.

The poem "archy declares war" from the lives and times of archy & mehitabel by Don Marquis is reprinted by permission of Doubleday & Co., Inc. Copyright 1927, 1930 by Doubleday & Co., Inc.; copyright 1916, 1917, 1919, 1921, 1922 by Sun Printing & Publishing Association. Copyright 1922, 1923, 1924, 1925 by New York Tribune, Inc. Copyright 1925, 1926 by P. F. Collier and Son Co.

The illustrations from the lives and times of archy & mehitabel are reprinted by permission of Doubleday & Co., Inc. Copyright 1927 (1930, illustrations) by George Herriman. Copyright 1927 (1930, illustrations) by Doubleday & Company, Inc.

The excerpt from The Sacred Beetle and Others by J. Henri Fabre, translated by Alexander Teixeira de Mattos, is reprinted by permission of Dodd, Mead & Co., Inc. Copyright 1918 by Dodd, Mead & Company. Copyright renewed 1946 by Geoffrey William Russell. Acknowledgment to Hughes Massie Ltd.

The excerpt from Leiningen Versus the Ants by Carl Stephenson is reprinted by permission of Ann Elmo Agency. Copyright by Carl Stephenson.

ISBN 0-913948-12-8

Library of Congress Catalog Card Number: 76-58898

Introduction
by John Neary

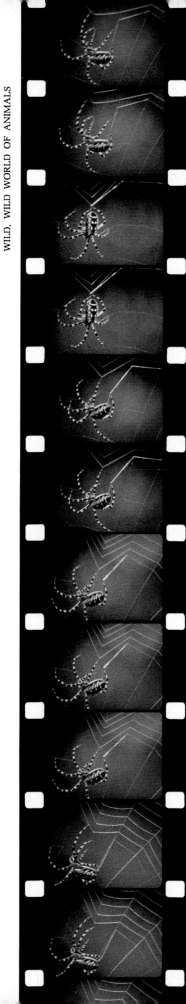

Mᴀɴ ɪꜱ ꜱᴀɪᴅ ᴛᴏ ᴅᴏᴍɪɴᴀᴛᴇ ᴛʜᴇ ᴇᴀʀᴛʜ, but the insects are the true lords of the planet, if only in sheer numbers. There are nearly four times as many species of insects as all other animals combined. Entomologists have identified 800,000 different insect species, and they agree that at least a million must exist. One conservative estimate of the total population of individual insects is a mind-boggling quintillion—1,000,000,000,000,000,000 tiny creatures that fly and burrow and crawl and swim almost everywhere on earth. In terms of evolutionary success, insects must be ranked as the undisputed champions.

They are the most ubiquitous of all animals and have adapted to environments where few other fauna can exist. There are insects living 20,000 feet high in the Himalayas, on the surface of the ocean, deep within the Arctic Circle, on the burning dunes of deserts and burrowed far underground. With the often unwitting assistance of man, insects have invaded worlds where there were no insects before, including the astronauts' space capsules; they have traveled across the seas to new environments, often with devastating results, as the migrations to America of the crop-destroying Japanese beetle and the forest-devouring European gypsy moth bear witness.

The class Insecta (from the Latin word meaning "sliced," a reference to bodies that are always segmented) belongs to the larger phylum Arthropoda (from the Greek for "joined feet"), along with other groups of invertebrates including three that are usually confused with insects: spiders, scorpions, mites and ticks (Arachnida); centipedes (Chilopoda) and millipedes (Diplopoda). Because of their close association with insects, these animals are examined in two sections of this book. True insects are distinguished by the organization of their bodies, which are divided into three distinct parts—a head, a thorax and an abdomen. All adult insects have six legs (spiders have eight, centipedes as many as 346); one pair of antennae for touching, smelling and hearing; mouths equipped with parts for chewing, piercing or sucking; and a tough, resilient external skeleton made of a flexible material called chitin. Nearly all insects have two compound eyes, although a few have none. There the family resemblances among insects end. Through eons of evolution, the insects have taken on a bewildering array of forms, colors, disguises and specializations to meet the demands of their changing ecosystems.

Like all the creatures of the earth, the insects have been part of a vast, ongoing experiment to discover what works and what does not. And they have found many more successful ways of surviving than the others that share the planet with them. For instance, some caterpillars have large imitation eyes on their sides that hoodwink would-be predators.

Other insects assumed the appearance of sticks or leaves or bird droppings as camouflage. In response to emerging opportunities, insects and related invertebrates developed weapons, skills and, among insects only, social systems. Very early in arthropod evolution segments consolidated into sections with special functions. Some legs became mouth parts—chewing in insects, pinching in arachnids. First termites, much later some wasps and bees, and all

8

A Guatemalan rain forest teems with insects, producing some of the world's largest, most spectacular specimens.

the ants came to live in family groups, most individuals losing their reproductive capacity to the advantage of the colony as a whole. In time, insects became skilled architects, papermakers, spinners of webs, agriculturists, potters, herders, even undertakers. They learned to enslave other insects, to make war, to manage nurseries. Most of them became masters of aerodynamics—the first and for 150 million years the only creatures on earth to grow wings and fly.

Flying enabled insects to escape their enemies and to move to more favorable environments, but it is only one of several factors contributing to their remarkable success story. Their relatively small size—among modern insects, the greatest wingspan, about 13 inches, is that of a South American moth; the smallest insect, an almost microscopic beetle, can easily crawl through the eye of a needle—has been another advantage, permitting them to escape enemies, wriggle into small places for food and utilize smaller habitats in far greater numbers than larger animals. The exoskeleton was another factor, a protective shield that also helped keep moisture in the body from evaporating, an obvious threat to such small animals.

The insects' particular system of metamorphosis, passing through several stages of development from egg to maturity, also helped them survive. The process usually permits the larva to live in one place and eat one kind of food and allows the adult to exploit other environments, foods and opportunities without mutually damaging competition. Through a flexible mode of reproduction, insects are able to delay egg hatching so that the process of maturing will culminate when the adult has the best chance of finding a mate. Insects have also found the means of survival in superabundant reproduction. The rapidity of their reproductive cycle and the overwhelming numbers of their offspring are virtual guarantees of survival. A queen bee can produce 600,000 fertile eggs in her lifetime, and a female housefly and her offspring have the capability of bringing forth a staggering 56 trillion descendants in a single summer.

Since man first appeared on earth, he has been engaged in unremitting conflict with the insects, which remain, significantly, the only animals that he

10

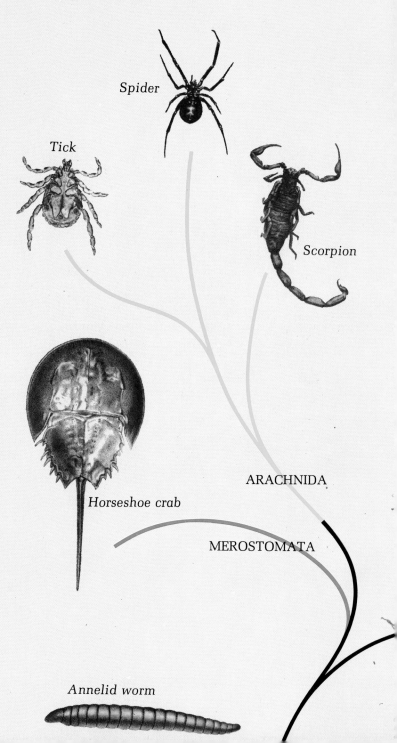

The animals discussed in this volume (yellow, red and green lines) are related to one another—and to others not covered in the book (blue lines). All are descended from a simple annelid, or segmented worm (bottom). About 600 million years ago, this evolutionary trunk (black line) branched; the left-hand branch led to the horseshoe crabs, and their terrestrial relatives, the scorpions and spiders. From the right-hand branch developed the crustaceans and their land-dwelling kin, the millipedes, centipedes and insects. Among the earliest flying insects, emerging some 320 million years ago, were giant dragonflies, some with wingspreads of 30 inches.

Spider

Tick

Scorpion

Horseshoe crab

ARACHNIDA

MEROSTOMATA

Annelid worm

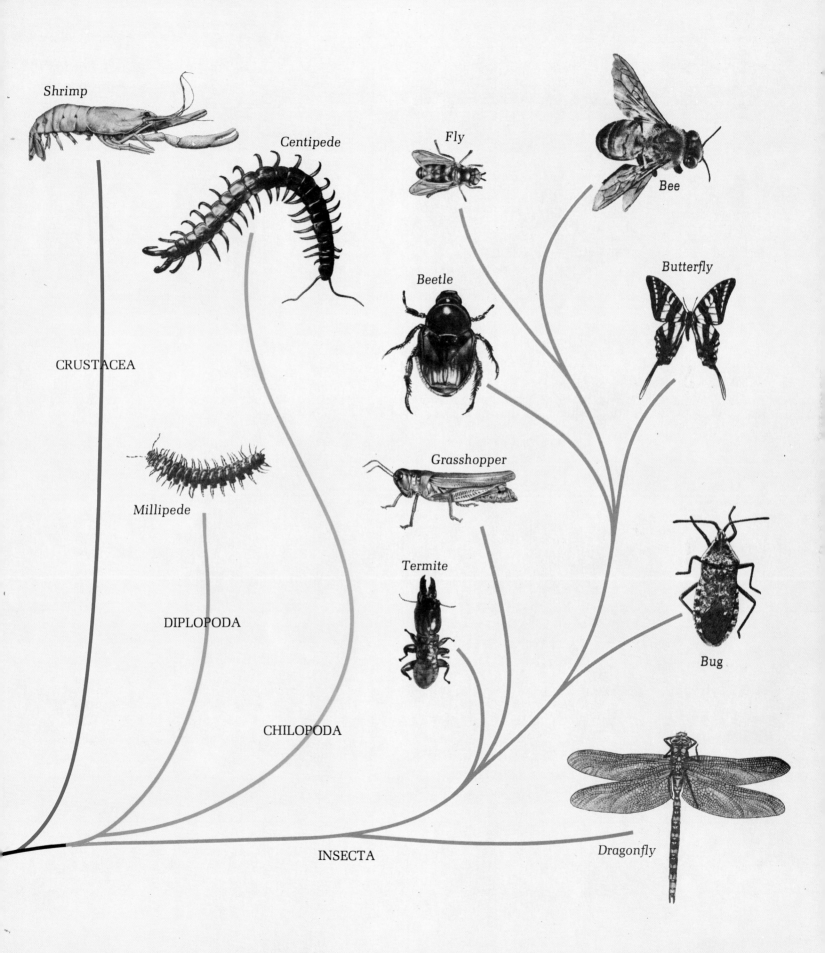

Shrimp

Centipede

Fly

Bee

Beetle

Butterfly

CRUSTACEA

Grasshopper

Millipede

DIPLOPODA

Termite

Bug

CHILOPODA

INSECTA

Dragonfly

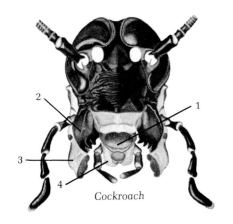

Cockroach

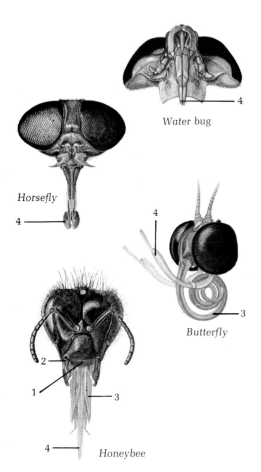

Water bug

Horsefly

Butterfly

Honeybee

Though adapted to serve specialized feeding needs, the mouthparts of most insects comprise "lips" called (1) the labium and (4) the labrum for closing the mouth, (2) mandibles for cutting and (3) maxillae for handling food. The cockroach retains all these pieces of equipment in its basic form. The water bug's mouth is built to pierce and suck; the horsefly is able to pierce prey and sponge up body juices. In the butterfly, the mouth is a highly specialized siphoning tube. The bee can both chew and suck up food.

has not been able to exterminate, effectively control, contain or tame. On the contrary, the insect pests have increased their numbers enormously and flourished in spite of all human efforts to extirpate them. They have invaded the homes of men and undermined their foundations. They have destroyed crops at an appalling rate—75 percent of one annual harvest in Kenya, for example—and have been the indirect cause of the starvation of multitudes. They have made vast areas uninhabitable, attacked and killed domestic animals and, as the carriers of deadly plagues and fevers, caused the deaths of millions of people and altered the course of history. A plague carried by lice wiped out 10 million people in India at the turn of the century. In the 1880s France abandoned work on the Panama Canal after 20,000 workers died from yellow fever carried by mosquitoes or, as a saying of the day had it, one man for every crosstie in the Panama Railroad.

A strong case can be made for some insects as useful and beneficial to mankind. Among them are the honeybee, producer of honey and wax and pollinator of flowers; the mayfly, an important item in the diet of game fish; and the ladybird beetle, which preys on crop-destroying insects. And it is indubitably true that without insects the flowers, fruits, vegetables, small mammals, fish and birds of the earth would be drastically reduced in numbers, if not exterminated. But the insects' role as destroyers has also created enormous problems for mankind. Even today, these problems are largely insoluble.

For a time in the recent past, pesticides seemed to be the answer. But in attempting to control the destructive insects with chemicals, men have not only polluted earth and water and killed off useful insects and other animals, but the effect has backlashed and brought back insect pests in renewed strength. Pesticides that were capable of wiping out one generation of insects have sometimes triggered adaptations in later generations, which acquired the ability to resist the chemicals. Entomologists reckon that of 500 insect species that are harmful to agriculture, 267 have become immune to DDT and some other insecticides.

In achieving their extraordinary ability to survive, insects have solved the problems of life in ways that set them dramatically apart from other animals.

But the solution depends not at all on intelligence; no reasoning ability whatever is present in insect brains no larger than the head of a finishing nail. "Instinct" is the word used to designate the mysterious, reflexive, ingrained response to stimuli, programmed at birth—never forgotten but never learned, either. To cite instinct, however, does not provide an answer. It merely labels another mystery: how and why these programmed responses are transmitted from generation to generation to generation and how they work.

Very gradually the mystery is being unlocked. Two new sciences—zoosemiotics, the study of animal communication, and population biology—have arisen. Workers in zoosemiotics have been able to identify a number of chemical signals, called pheromones, that are transmitted from bee to bee, from ant to ant, from mother wasp to wasp larva, which communicate information and elicit responses. The discovery is not altogether new. In 1609 Charles Butler wrote in *The Feminine Monarchie,* "When you are stung, or any in the company, yea though a Bee have strike but your clothes, specially in hot weather, you have best be packing as fast as you can: for the other Bees smelling the ranke flavor of the poison cast out with the sting will come about you thick as haile."

Decidedly new, however, is the prospect that modern observers, equipped with sophisticated detecting apparatus, can penetrate the insects' chemical code and crack it. Since Charles Butler first noticed that bees act in concert, keen observation has revealed the meaning of a curious bee dance whose patterns are directions to nectar sources for the rest of the hive. The day may come when researchers will rear larvae just as bees do, determining their roles as queens or workers by varying food, pheromone and hormone intake. Entomologists also hope that predictable responses can be evolved in isolated insects by submitting them to artificial chemical and physical environments, including nests constructed so realistically that insects will respond to the laboratory-built fakes just as they would to the nests they build for themselves. The first steps have already been taken toward achieving those goals. Many pheromones have been identified, and some have been put to use controlling agricultural pests and disease carriers by manipulating life cycles, stunting development or accelerating mating to abort reproduction or cause it to take place when eggs and larvae will freeze or starve to death.

The prospect of subduing the insect world is heady, but it raises some troubling questions, and it is by no means certain. Even as the researchers learn more about insects and attempt to control them, the insects may evolve methods of avoiding control, just as they overcame DDT. For the possibility remains strong that insects will forever resist the ultimate penetration of their mysteries. Maurice Maeterlinck, the mystical Belgian author who was also a dedicated amateur entomologist, expressed the problem eloquently. "Something in the insect," he wrote, "seems to be alien to the habits, morals and psychology of this world, as if it has come from some other planet, more monstrous, more energetic, more insensate, more atrocious, more infernal than our own."

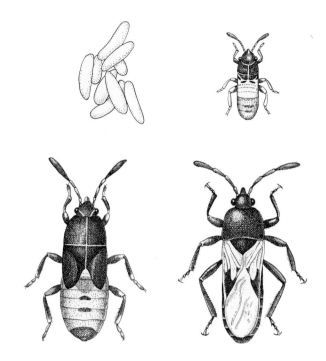

The drawings above illustrate the development of a chinch bug from egg (top, left) to adult (bottom, right). Known as incomplete metamorphosis, the process is characterized by the marked resemblance of the newly hatched nymph, or young (top, right), to the adult. The nymph lacks only wings and reproductive organs, which begin to appear sometime after the third molt (bottom, left). The chinch bug undergoes a total of five molts between its egg and adult stages.

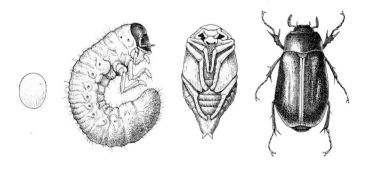

The life stages of a beetle are illustrated above. Beetles undergo complete metamorphosis, a four-stage process of development. It begins with the egg (left), which hatches the larva (second from left); the pupa (second from right) develops into the adult (right). The insect changes its appearance dramatically in each stage. As a larva, it spends almost all of its time in search of food. In contrast, the incipient beetle eats nothing at all during the pupal stage, a quiescent period of radical change when structures that characterize the adult, such as wing pads, are formed.

Spiders

An ancient Greek myth tells of a lovely Lydian maid, Arachne, a weaver whose art was so intricate and beautiful that she challenged the goddess Athene herself to a contest at the loom. When Athene responded by destroying Arachne's weavings, the stricken girl hanged herself. Athene, perhaps remorseful, perhaps out of spite, thereupon changed the dead maiden into a spider, forevermore to weave her gossamer tapestries as traps for prey less wary than a goddess.

The spider and its relatives, the scorpions, mites and ticks, keep the old name Arachnida, an order whose members range in size from a microscopic mite to a tarantula, whose body is five inches long and whose legs span eight inches. Arachnids, like their six-legged cousins the insects, are arthropods—the evolutionary descendants of sea-dwelling creatures called trilobites. The first known land animal was a scorpion; it appeared some 400 million years ago. In the eons since, arachnids have evolved into no fewer than 54,590 species, flourishing in virtually every place on earth that can support life—from scorching desert to chill mountain slopes. Some even spend their lives under water, like *Argyroneta aquatica,* a skin-diving spider (page 24) that carries a bubble of air beneath the surface, where it eats, rests and mates within a silk diving bell.

The world's spiders are carnivores, truly as deadly as they appear but usually only to creatures on their own scale. For all the widespread fear and revulsion they provoke, and despite the fact that almost all are venomous, few spiders are capable of causing man any serious or lasting harm. Though the black widow and its cousins are as notorious as the spiders with the most toxic venom in North America, even they attack people only in self-defense, and their bite is estimated to cause death in less than 5 percent of those bitten.

To trap their prey, most spiders rely on webs, but the variety of their silken snares is nearly as great as the widely differing creatures themselves. Some rig sticky traps above their webs to help ensure a catch. One species employs silk the way an angler uses line and lure, casting it off into the air to catch whatever passes by. Silk is produced by hundreds of glands inside the spider's body and is emitted through spinning tubes connected to the glands. Most of these tubes are located at the end of tiny fingerlike spinnerets on the spider's abdomen. The spider spins many different silks, effortlessly blending the flow from different spinning tubes as it weaves. When it chooses it can coat the strands with glue from which it protects itself by virtue of an oily secretion.

Among the various types of silk that spiders can produce are thick strands for the dragline by which the spider lowers itself from a tree limb or a lampshade to seek a new lair; numerous fine threads for the attachment device that anchors the dragline; viscous and elastic fibers for the orb-weaver's net; and the gossamer bands and films in which spiders swathe their victims and encase their eggs. Although none can produce all those kinds of silk, every spider can make at least three types. Baby spiderlings also weave, making tiny copies of their mother's webs. Mature males are able to spin but generally only females continue the art into adulthood.

Not all spiders weave webs: Wolf spiders stalk their quarry, running in for the kill; crab spiders lie in wait for an unwary meal to pass by; jumping spiders, among the few arachnids that possess good vision—most rely on a keen sense of touch—spy out their victims and then pounce. Spiders kill or paralyze their prey swiftly, stabbing with a pair of appendages called *chelicerae,* which have evolved into hollow, daggerlike fangs that inject a powerful venom. Having prepared the meal, a spider digests it before ingesting it, pumping a secretion into the victim's body that liquefies body tissues; the spider then sucks out the pre-digested juices.

Other arachnids have developed different but equally effective techniques of predation. The scorpions have powerful pincers that crush and hold prey while injecting the venom through its tail-mounted sting. Some mites and their larger relatives, ticks, obtain a purchase on a host with barbed and sucking mouth parts, so sharp that victims are often not even aware of their presence until the animals' blood-gorged bodies are noticed.

Ticks can transmit diseases, such as tularemia and relapsing fever, to people and livestock by their bites and are far more harmful to man than any of their arachnid kin. Spiders, on the other hand, are of enormous value to man, helping prevent his house, garden and greenhouse—his whole world—from becoming overrun by insects. According to one conservative estimate, spiders, by merely living at their customary population density of two and a quarter million to one acre of grass, kill some 200 trillion insects a year in England and Wales alone.

Spiny spider

Signatures in Silk

All spiders are capable of manufacturing silk, although not all are web-spinners. For those species that do construct webs, however, the silken networks are trademarks—nearly as reliable as anatomical characteristics in identifying a family of spiders. The master weavers among the spiders are the araneids, whose unmistakable orb webs (left) have distinctive cartwheel designs that often measure over a foot in diameter and are unsurpassed in delicacy.

The multilevel construction of the web of *Linyphia communis* (below) has led some scientists to refer to its creator as the "bowl and doily" spider. Usually found on low bushes, these webs consist of a shallow silk cup beneath which is stretched an almost flat sheet of threads—the bowl and its doily. In addition, a maze of silk extends above the bowl, and the entire structure is secured to nearby twigs or stems by strong anchor lines. Insects that fly too close to the web are tripped by the lines and plummet to the center of the bowl, where the spider lies in wait with the doily underneath to catch any spillovers.

Perched on the stem of a plant, a spider spins a thick strand of silk. Glands inside the spider's body produce a liquid substance called fibroin that hardens into thread as it is drawn from the spider's body. The silk is emitted through flexible protuberances on the spider's abdomen called spinnerets. These spinning organs can produce threads of different thicknesses, as well as fibers that are either dry or sticky. As a group, spiders are capable of manufacturing seven different types of silk, though no single species can produce all seven. The orb-weaving spiders, which are among the most talented spinners, can make five different kinds. Despite its fineness, spider silk is extremely strong, surpassed in tensile strength by no other natural fibers.

While most of the silk spiders spin is used to trap prey, there are other weblike structures with completely different uses. The skein of woven silk shown below is a spider's retreat, the place where the spinner waits until a victim blunders into a silken trap that is usually nearby. The retreat is connected to the trap web by strands of silk. The struggles of a trapped insect create vibrations, which are transmitted like a telegraphed message, an unmistakable announcement that "dinner is served."

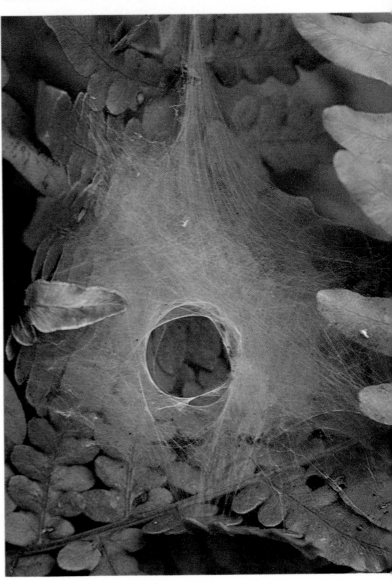

Midnight Cowboy

The sequence of pictures on these pages illustrates the hunting techniques of the ogre-faced spider, which catches its prey by means of a silk net that it casts over the victim. At left, the spider is suspended on a few supporting threads and spins the tangle of dry threads that makes up its trap. The spider holds the completed net, as shown in the picture below, with its forelegs, ready to cast. The net is extremely elastic and can accommodate victims of varying sizes, but each net can be used only once. The ogre-face does its net-casting only at night. It spends the day sleeping, its drab color and stretched-out position disguising it as a twig.

Having spied a likely target, an ogre-faced spider flings its net over the victim, which soon becomes tangled in the net's crisscross of threads (left). The insect is immediately swathed in a cocoon of silk (below) that immobilizes it and permits the spider to eat at its leisure.

Torrent of Spiderlings

Spiders are often prolific. Although most produce no more than 100 and some lay only two eggs at a time, others lay as many as 3,000. The eggs are deposited in masses, each protected with a strong silk coating or egg sac, which many spider mothers tie to a secure mooring and then die, leaving the young to fend for themselves. In contrast, other females, such as the attentive pisaurids, carry their egg sacs with them until the young are ready to hatch. They then weave a nursery web and guard the tiny offspring (opposite) until they are old enough to live independently.

Another vigilant mother is the wolf spider. She drags her egg sac behind her as she hunts for food. Once the eggs hatch, the young cluster on her back (below) until they are about a week old.

Most spiderlings literally launch themselves out into the world by "ballooning." The youngster climbs to the top of a twig or fence post, faces into the wind and unreels a thread of silk, which is picked up by air currents. As the line gets longer, the wind lifts the spider off its perch, and the creature then drifts off like a kite.

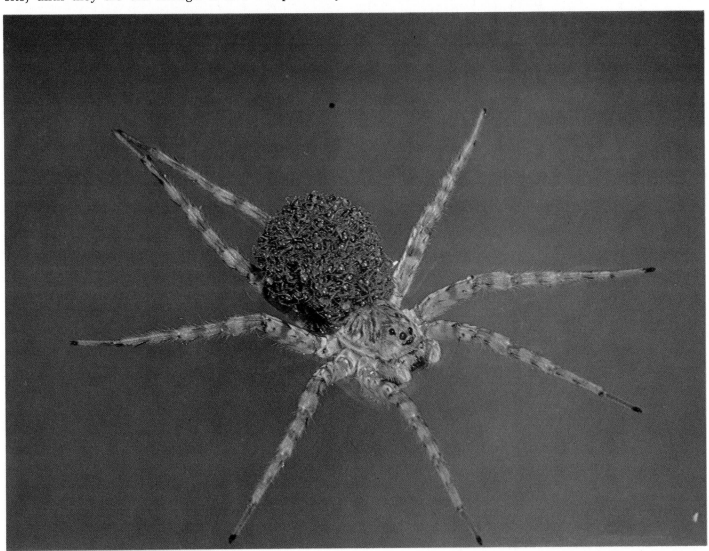

Aquacade

Many spiders trap their food in webs, but numerous species use very different, specialized means to hunt quarry and elude enemies. Two remarkable examples are the fishing spider, *Dolomedes triton* (opposite), and the diving spider, *Argyroneta aquatica* (below). The fishing spider has the best of two worlds. Found in marshy areas, it is equally at home on land and in the water. Among spiders, it has a rare ability to run across the surface of the water in pursuit of insects, its primary sustenance, as well as an occasional tadpole or minnow. When frightened, the fishing spider dives beneath the surface and is able to stay submerged for over an hour.

Found only in northern Europe, the diving spider is an even more talented submariner, spending almost its entire life underwater. But like all spiders, it is air-breathing. To maintain a supply of oxygen, *Argyroneta* constructs a diving bell that it uses as an air trap. It starts by spinning a sheet of silk and anchoring it to an aquatic plant. The spider then rises to the surface and captures an air bubble, which it gingerly maneuvers under the silk to form an air-filled pouch. As the oxygen is used up, the spider rises to the surface to get new bubbles. The frequency of these trips depends on how active the spider is. One bubble may provide enough air to last a resting spider several hours.

Legs outstretched, a fishing spider, Dolomedes triton, *floats placidly on the water's surface. This beautiful spider is often called the six-dotted Dolomedes because of the six dark spots on its back (four are visible in this photograph). Widespread in North America, this spider hides under leaves when threatened, riding back to the surface on an air bubble held like a pontoon beneath its body.*

Disappearing Acts

Spiders employ a variety of stratagems to protect themselves from predators or to conceal themselves from potential prey. A number of species have become masters of deception. Some have perfected a natural camouflage called cryptic coloration that enables them to blend into the background, where they hide or lie in wait. Others bear a protective resemblance to inert objects common in the environment such as lichen (left) or bird droppings.

This differs from mimicry. A mimic spider assumes the physical appearance of a different, less vulnerable animal. Some spiders go undetected by seeking refuge in cover provided by their surroundings, such as rocky crevices or leaves. If disturbed, however, a spider will quickly abandon its concealment or drop its assumed identity and simply flee for its life.

The mottled colors of the bark spider (above) are almost exactly like the lichen-covered bark of the tree on which it waits for prey. The patch on the leaf at right, which looks like bird excrement, is actually the extraordinary disguise of the spider known as Phrysarachne. The spider's blotchy black-and-white markings combine with the irregular patches of silk it spreads on the leaf to complete the camouflage.

26

Leaf-rolling (above) is a trait of several groups of spiders. These leaflike tubes are used as hiding places for the spiders as well as retreats in which they lay their eggs. For the spider at right, mimicking an ant can be a lifesaving tactic against predators. The spider sometimes embellishes the performance by waving its front legs like antennae.

Come into My Parlor

As a group, spiders have more costume variations than any Paris fashion show. But because they are, undeservedly, among the most feared of nature's creatures, few people get close enough to take a good look at their often dazzling appearance. The lynx spider at left is one of the most attractive, with a bright green body splashed by small red dots and long legs covered with thin black spines. Like its feline namesake, the lynx spider is a hunter that patiently stalks its prey before leaping on it for the kill.

The bulbous, speckled body below belongs to the shamrock spider. This arachnid spins a two-and-one-half-foot-wide orb web and then waits in a silken retreat nearby for its next meal to come along. The furry fellow opposite is a jumping spider, so called because of its ability to leap many times its own length in pursuit of prey. The jumping spider can identify friend, foe or prey as far away as 12 inches—a record for farsightedness in the spider world.

Although most spiders have eight eyes, their sense of sight varies greatly. The lynx spider (above) is a diurnal hunter and must rely heavily on its vision for catching prey. Like most other spiders, the shamrock spider (right) is myopic. It uses a web as a trap and depends almost entirely on its sense of touch to reach and administer the coup de grâce to its quarry.

The Widow's Bite

Of the dozen-odd spiders that pose a threat to man, the black widow is among the most dangerous. The male of the species is small and virtually harmless, but the female is armed with a venom that, drop for drop, is more potent than a rattlesnake's. The spider, shown above in her characteristic upside-down position, shows off the distinctive red hourglass marking on her abdomen. Although she packs a powerful bite, the female black widow is not as bloodthirsty as her name implies. Contrary to popular belief, she does not always kill the male after mating, although like most female spiders she will resort to eating her own kind when she is hungry.

During courtship the male approaches her web with understandable caution. If she is receptive there is a mutual exchange of vibrations played out on the threads of her web; then the male slowly makes his way to the female. With her consent he binds her loosely with silk to immobilize her before the transfer of sperm takes place. Once the transfer is completed, the female breaks her bonds—a rapid process but one that gives the male just enough time to make his getaway from a mate that may be too hungry to resist eating him.

A male black widow (below) performs his only mission in life—the risky business of mating with a deadly female twice his size. A female (right) jealously guards the silk sacs containing the eggs she has just laid. The sacs are watertight and strong enough to protect the eggs against most predators. After a gestation period that lasts as long as 30 days in cool climates, the spiderlings tear the casing and emerge. They are now at their most vulnerable and run the risk of falling prey to insects, to their own mother and particularly to one another.

Hairy and Scary

Nightmare visions with hairy, sprawling limbs, tarantulas are the giants among spiders. They are commonly encountered in the southwestern United States, Mexico and Central and South America and look much like the horrendous European wolf spider, *Lycosa tarentula*, whose bite was once thought to cause "tarentism," a fatal condition that could supposedly be cured only by dancing a frantic tarantella. The tarantulas of the American Southwest, whose bodies are up to three inches long, spend the day in underground burrows and hunt at night. Their powerful venom is not harmful to man, but it can paralyze small mammals and reptiles, although tarantulas dine mainly on insects.

It takes about 10 years and some 15 molts for a North American tarantula to reach adult size. The sexes are indistinguishable until after the last molt, when the male pedipalps—leglike parts located between the jaws and the front legs—develop enlarged tips that are used in reproduction. The male dies shortly after mating. The female deposits her eggs in a hammock of silk she has spun in her burrow. Soon after they hatch, the young crawl away to build burrows of their own, but their mother survives long after their departure, often living a quarter of a century.

Larger than its Pepsis wasp adversary (above), the nearsighted tarantula is nevertheless at a disadvantage against the keen-sighted wasp. The Honduran tarantula (right) has had more success in capturing a garter snake, an unusual victim.

Antique Stinger

The earliest of the terrestrial arachnids, scorpions have remained virtually unchanged for millions of years. They are generally found in the warmer areas of the world, especially around deserts, where they escape the drying effects of the sun by remaining under cover during the day, hiding in rocky cracks and crevices or in two- to three-foot burrows they dig with their front legs. At night they leave their subterranean homes and wait nearby for an unwary spider, beetle or cockroach to wander within reach.

The scorpion uses the sting at the end of its tail (opposite) only on victims that are quite large or put up a struggle; those that do not resist are simply torn to pieces with sharp mouth parts and eaten. The less tractable prey is held firmly in place by the scorpion's pincers and immobilized by a quick stab of the sting, which the scorpion swings forward over its head.

Mating between scorpions starts with an elaborate courtship. Tails upturned and intertwined, male and female perform a kind of tango that ends with the male secreting a spermatophore, or packet of sperm, that is ultimately transferred to the female. Mating occasionally ends with the female paralyzing and devouring her mate, though this outcome is extremely rare. Scorpions are timid creatures that strike out only when threatened. Most of the 700 species are not fatal to man, their stings producing, at worst, pain followed by numbness, swelling and fever.

After giving birth, the female scorpion carries her family on her back (above), a habit she shares with her cousin the wolf spider. The young scorpions remain with their mother until after their first molt. Only after their seventh or eighth molt, a development period of about five years, do they reach maturity. The largest species, the African emperor scorpion (left), grows to a length of eight inches.

The Courtship of the Scorpion

by Jean Henri Fabre

A French physicist who abandoned a teaching career at the age of 50 to pursue his lifelong interest in entomology, Fabre was one of the first scientific writers to publish popular studies of small creatures. His 10-volume Souvenirs Entomologiques, *written between 1869 and 1907, is a meticulous and lively account of the insects and arachnids in the neighborhood of his home in southern France. The following selection records the nuptial rites of captive scorpions in Fabre's backyard. It begins with the male scorpion courting a likely-looking mate by standing on his head, and ends in a grim* danse macabre.

25th April, 1904.—Hullo! What is this, something I have not yet seen? My eyes, ever on the watch, look upon the affair for the first time. Two Scorpions face each other, with claws outstretched and fingers clasped. It is a question of a friendly grasp of the hand and not the prelude to a battle, for the two partners are behaving to each other in the most peaceful way. There is one of either sex. One is paunchy and browner than the other: this is the female; the other is comparatively slim and pale: this is the male. With their tails prettily curled, the couple stroll with measured steps along the pane. The male is ahead and walks backwards, without jolt or jerk, without any resistance to overcome. The female follows obediently, clasped by her finger-tips and face to face with her leader.

The stroll is interrupted by halts that do not affect the method of conjunction; it is resumed, now here, now there, from end to end of the enclosure. Nothing shows the object which the strollers have in view. They loiter, they dawdle, they most certainly exchange ogling glances. Even so in my village, on Sundays, after vespers, do the youth of both sexes saunter along the hedges, every Jack with his Jill.

Often they tack about. It is always the male who decides which fresh direction the pair shall take. Without releasing her hands, he turns gracefully to the left or right about and places himself side by side with companion. Then, for a moment, with tail laid flat, he strokes her spine. The other stands motionless, impassive.

For over an hour, without tiring, I watch these interminable comings and goings. A part of the household lends me its eyes in the presence of the strange sight which no one in the world has yet seen, at least with a vision capable of observing. In spite of the lateness of the hour, which upsets all our habits, our attention is concentrated and no essential thing escapes us.

At last, about ten o'clock, something happens. The male has hit upon a potsherd whose shelter seems to suit him. He releases his companion with one hand, with one alone, and continuing to hold her with the other, he scratches with his legs and sweeps with his tail. A grotto opens. He enters and, slowly, without violence, drags the patient Scorpioness after him. Soon both have disappeared. A plug of sand closes the dwelling. The couple are at home.

To disturb them would be a blunder: I should be interfering too soon, at an inopportune moment, if I tried at once to see what was happening below. The preliminary stages may last for the best part of the night; and it does not do for me, who have turned eighty, to sit up so late. I feel my legs giving way; and my eyes seem full of sand.

All night long I dream of Scorpions. They crawl under my bedclothes, they pass over my face; and I am not particularly excited, so many curious things do I see in my imagination. The next morning, at daybreak, I lift the stoneware. The female is alone. Of the male there is no trace, either in the home or in the neighbourhood. First disappointment, to be followed by many others.

10th May.—It is nearly seven o'clock in the evening; the sky is overcast with signs of an approaching shower. Under one of the potsherds is a motionless couple, face to face, with linked fingers. Cautiously I raise the potsherd and leave the occupants uncovered, so as to study the consequences of the interview at my ease. The darkness of the night falls and nothing, it seems to me, will disturb the calm of the home deprived of its roof. A sharp shower compels me to retire. They, under the lid of the cage, have no need to take shelter against the rain. What will they do, left to their business as they are but deprived of a canopy to their alcove?

An hour later, the rain ceases and I return to my Scorpions. They are gone. They have taken up their abode under a neighbouring tile. Still with their fingers linked, the female is outside and the male indoors, preparing the home. At intervals of ten minutes, the members of my family relieve one another so as not to lose the exact moment of the pairing, which appears to be imminent. Wasted pains: at eight o'clock, it being now quite dark, the couple, dissatisfied with the spot, set out on a fresh ramble, hand in hand, and go prospecting elsewhere. The male, walking backwards, leads the way, chooses the dwelling as he pleases; the female follows with docility. It is an exact repetition of what I saw on the 25th of April.

At last a tile is found to suit them. The male goes in first but this time neither hand releases his companion for a moment. The nuptial chamber is prepared with a few sweeps of the tail. Gently drawn towards him, the Scorpioness enters in the wake of her guide.

I visit them a couple of hours later, thinking that I've given them time enough to finish their preparations. I lift the potsherd. They are there in the same posture, face to face and hand in hand. I shall see no more today.

The next day, nothing new either. Each sits confronting the other, meditatively. Without stirring a limb, the gossips, holding each other by the finger-tips, continue their endless interview under the tile. In the evening, at sunset, after sitting linked together for four-and-twenty hours, the couple separate. He goes away from the tile, she remains; and matters have not advanced by an inch.

This observation gives us two facts to remember. After the stroll to celebrate the betrothal, the couple need the mystery and quiet of a shelter. Never would the nuptials be consummated in the open air, amid the bustling crowd, in sight of all. Remove the roof of the house, by night or day, with all possible discretion; and the husband and wife, who seem absorbed in meditation, march off in search of another spot. Also, the sojourn under the cover of a stone is a long one; we have just seen it spun out to twenty-four hours and even then without a decisive result.

12th May.—What will this evening's sitting teach us? The weather is calm and hot, favourable to nocturnal pastimes. A couple has been formed; how things began I do not know. This time the male is greatly inferior to his corpulent mate. Nevertheless, the skinny wight performs his duty gallantly. Walking backwards, according to rule, with his tail rolled trumpetwise, he marches the fat Scorpioness around the glass ramparts. After one circuit follows another, sometimes in the same, sometimes in the opposite direction.

Pauses are frequent. Then the foreheads touch, bend a little to left and right, as if the two were whispering in each other's ears. The little fore-legs flutter in feverish caresses. What are they saying to each other? How shall we translate their silent epithalamium into words?

The whole household turns out to see this curious team, which our presence in no way disturbs. The pair are

pronounced to be "pretty"; and the expression is not exaggerated. Semi-translucent and shining in the light of the lantern, they seem carved out of a block of amber. Their arms outstretched, their tails rolled into graceful spirals, they wander on with a slow movement and with measured tread.

Nothing puts them out. Should some vagabond, taking the evening air and keeping to the wall like themselves, meet them on their way, he stands aside—for he understands these delicate matters—and leaves them a free passage. Lastly, the shelter of a tile receives the strolling pair, the male entering first and backwards: that goes without saying. It is nine o'clock.

The idyll of the evening is followed, during the night, by a hideous tragedy. Next morning, we find the Scorpioness under the potsherd of the previous day. The little male is by her side, but slain, and more or less devoured. He lacks the head, a claw, a pair of legs. I place the corpse in the open, on the threshold of the home. All day long, the recluse does not touch it. When night returns, she goes out and, meeting the deceased on her passage, carries him off to a distance to give him a decent funeral, that is to finish eating him.

This act of cannibalism agrees with what the open-air colony showed me last year. From time to time, I would find, under the stones, a pot-bellied female making a comfortable ritual meal off her companion of the night. I suspected that the male, if he did not break loose in time, once his functions were fulfilled, was devoured, wholly or partly, according to the matron's appetite. I now have the certain proof before my eyes. Yesterday, I saw the couple enter their home after their usual preliminary, the stroll; and, this morning, under the same tile, at the moment of my visit, the bride is consuming her mate.

Centipedes and Millipedes

Four hundred and fifty million years ago—150 million years before the insects and their kin became as well established and widespread as they are today—a simple creature called an isopod may have lived in the shallow reaches of a pond. As the water in the pond rose and fell, flooded and evaporated, the isopod, a descendant of segmented worms called annelids that are believed to have been the precursors of all the insects and their relatives, somehow found a way to survive the dry spells. Thus it became a terrestrial creature.

That is an educated theory of the origin of two related but quite distinct classes of invertebrates—the Chilopoda, the centipedes, and the Diplopoda, the millipedes. These curious, primitive animals provide a flashback glimpse of creatures as they were in the dawn of life on land. A glance at their bodies reveals how they evolved more clearly than is the case with most present-day creatures. Evolution from a simple segmented worm into a centipede or a millipede, with the head and mouth parts of an insect, is an extraordinary leap indeed but one that is readily discernible and comparatively simple as evolutionary changes go.

By far the more active of the two classes is the centipede, with its limber, flattened body and a pair of legs attached to each of its body segments—sometimes as many as 173

pairs, sometimes as few as 15. Moving very quickly in a flowing motion, the centipede hunts for other creatures, including cockroaches, beetles and earthworms. Often it takes on that fearsome evolutionary antique, the scorpion—and wins. The centipede bites man, too, though only in self-defense, and while the tiny wound may be painful, only the bite of a large centipede can do serious harm.

The 3,000 species of centipedes (about 100 inhabit the United States) range from less than an inch in length to nearly a foot. The *Scolopendra gigantea* of Central America, believed to be the largest species, is 10½ inches long and an inch wide and eats lizards and mice. Despite the unappetizing appearance of centipedes, some South American Indians eat them with relish, after carefully removing their poisonous claws.

Most centipedes have simple eyes and photosensitive bodies that help them avoid the light that would expose them to predators. Experiments in which the centipedes' eyes were covered with paint demonstrated they can still sense light without being able to see it. One centipede, *Geophilus electricus,* is phosphorescent and leaves glowing trails that are capable of stinging a pursuer.

Reproduction among most centipedes does not involve copulation. The male deposits a sperm packet on the

ground, which the female thereupon takes up and stores for later fertilization of the egg. The females of some species make underground nurseries to contain their eggs, guarding them until they hatch, licking them to prevent the growth of parasitical fungi—and remaining alert lest a passing male eat them. The young emerge from the egg with only seven body segments, adding the remainder to their bodies as they molt.

Though millipedes, the so-called thousand-leggers, generally have a greater number of legs than centipedes, they cannot move as quickly as centipedes can and have had to forgo the role of hunter. Instead they feed on decomposing vegetable matter. Unlike the centipede, the millipede's body segments are fused into pairs, which causes each functioning segment of its body to appear to have two pairs of legs. Also unlike the centipede, the millipede's body is usually cylindrical and is covered by a hard shell.

Lacking the poisonous fangs of centipedes, some millipedes defend themselves by simply curling up in a tight spiral to thwart potential predators. Others have developed a formidable system of chemical warfare. Along each side of certain millipedes, like the gunports on a frigate, is a line of minute vents, with one on almost every segment of the wormlike body. Each vent is connected by a duct to a two-chambered internal gland. In the upper reservoir of the gland is a substance that, when released into the lower chamber to mix with an enzyme contained there, produces a deadly gas—hydrogen cyanide. Laboratory study of these millipedes has revealed that the creatures have a fine-tuned fire-control system for their artillery, releasing gas from ports only in the area of the body that is most threatened with attack by a predator. But if the millipede known as the *Apheloria corrugata* is handled, for instance, or if it is attacked by a number of predators, such as an army of ants, it lets go with a broadside volley from both sides and slithers away, leaving in its wake a lingering cloud of poison gas. And even when its built-in poison arsenal is temporarily exhausted, the millipede still has a second line of defense—a coating of toxic benzaldehyde on its body that repels persistent attackers.

Having uncovered the secrets of the millipede's complex defense system, scientists remain confronted with one puzzling question: How does the millipede manage to survive its own defense? Even when placed in a closed jar—and millipedes tend to prefer tightly enclosed places as natural habitats—filled with poisonous fumes, the thousand-leggers suffer no harm. The explanation for their immunity is still a scientific mystery.

Centipede

Dragonflies and Damselflies

Like the precursors of all other animals, the ancestors of insects were creatures of the sea, and a few species of bugs, moths, beetles and flies have re-entered the watery world of their origin to become more or less aquatic again. But three orders—the dragonflies, mayflies and stoneflies—with more than 7,600 species, have carried this reversion to an extreme: All their members spend most of their lives under water, to emerge in a relatively brief adulthood as flying creatures. The mature aquatic insects are a familiar sight, many flashing like tiny hovercraft over the surface of ponds and streams; but their adult phase is short, amounting to only a few summer weeks—or, in the case of mayflies, hours. In their immature stages, the aquatic insects spend from one to five years under water, breathing through gills and molting as often as 33 times before they take to the air.

In reverting to their watery environment, the aquatic insects have shown a remarkable adaptability. They are found all over the world, in frigid mountain streams and in hot springs with temperatures as high as 120° F., in torrential rivers and stagnant pools and brackish tidal swamps. When immature, some spend their lives precariously on the brinks of waterfalls; others are hatched in the water held inside the bucketlike hearts of bromeliad plants, high in the canopies of tropical rain forests.

Dragonflies and damselflies are the most spectacular of the three orders. Most have four iridescent wings; many have jewellike markings, and all share an undeservedly evil reputation. From primitive times they have been called creatures of the devil, with colloquial names such as horse-stingers, darning needles and snake doctors. Their tails are said to be tipped with poison stingers or needles, and legend has it that the "darning needles" can sew up the mouths of fibbing children. In fact, dragonflies are harmless to humans.

Although damselflies are weak fliers, dragonflies are among the fastest, most skillful of all airborne creatures. Individuals have been clocked at 35 miles per hour. Some species are long-distance travelers and have appeared on the decks of ships 200 miles from shore.

As nymphs, dragonflies are insatiable predators, feeding on other insects, tadpoles and small fish (in some fisheries they are regarded as a major menace to the fry). They are equipped with a grotesque lower jaw that serves to pinion prey and folds neatly under the mouth when not in use. Dragonfly adults use their legs to form a basket to scoop up midges, flies and other small insects (including other dragonflies). They often consume their prey in midair as they fly or hover, without bothering to search for a perch on which to feed.

Apart from the dragonfly, most of these insects are nonpredatory in their aquatic stages, subsisting on plankton and underwater vegetation. Since they are eaten in turn by fish, frogs and other larger animals, they form the first link in the food chain. How important that link is to the natural order was dramatically demonstrated when pollution in Lake Erie all but destroyed the mayfly population. With their primary food source gone, large numbers of the fish in the lake also disappeared.

Stoneflies take their name from the rocks they live under in fast-flowing streams. Their presence in a stream is widely accepted as a sign that the water is potable, and fishermen, uncovering a few under overturned stones, will unhesitatingly drink the water.

Mayflies are known to fishermen the world over for their spectacular "nuptial dances," when the pale adults rise over the water in great clouds of hundreds of thousands. Their brief lives as flying insects last no longer than a day or two and often only a few hours. In some areas the dead and dying mayflies have been known to pile up in great drifts, creating traffic hazards, snuffing out campfires and blackening streetlights. Although many of them do make their appearance during the month of May, they can, and do, rise during any of the warmer months.

The nuptial flights consist mainly of male mayflies, which alternately drift up and down with the air currents. When a female appears, a male detaches himself from the flight and mates with her. Her body is literally an airborne egg sac, crammed with hundreds of eggs, from the back of her head to the tip of her tail.

In the last act of the drama the male falls to his death, and the female has only enough time left to release her fertilized eggs on water. How she does this differs among species. After mating over a brook, for example, she may flutter upstream like a ballerina, then settle on the surface and, drifting downstream, deposit a ball of eggs, then flutter upstream again to release another clutch and then another. On contact with the water, each egg spins out tiny threads that anchor it securely to the river bottom or to submerged vegetation. When the female has delivered all of her eggs—as many as 600 or 700—to the water, she spreads her wings and dies, floating downstream on the surface and disappearing.

Damselfly

Keen-eyed Aviators

Although living from one to five years in the water before emerging as aviators, the brilliant-hued members of the order Odonata, such as the dragonfly (below) and the damselfly (left), demonstrate an exceptional knack for flying. Most species have distinctive flight patterns, some staying near the ground and landing frequently, others soaring at great heights above the treetops, while still others maintain a constant vigil over a stretch of river or stream, patrolling it with the regularity of a policeman on a beat.

Because they consume multitudes of such insect pests as mosquitoes, midges, gnats and flies—occasionally along with their own fellow creatures—most of the 4,500 known species of dragonflies and damselflies are considered beneficial to man.

In mating, damselflies must strike the awkward pose shown at left because of the unique location of the Odonata male's reproductive organs. They are positioned toward the front of the body in the second segment of the abdomen. While the female (on the bottom) curves her body beneath his, he grasps her by the back of the neck with posterior abdominal appendages.

The bulging compound eyes of the dragonfly, the most highly developed eyes in the insect world, not only equip it perfectly for its role as a midair hunter but also help protect it from predators. The compound eye is made up of some 28,000 six-sided facets; each is a self-contained visual system equipped with a lens, a light-transmitting apparatus and light-sensitive retinal cells. Though each facet registers only a fragment of the total scene, they all work in combination to provide a visual angle of nearly 180° and a reasonably sharp mosaiclike picture. The dragonfly's vision is keen enough, according to some entomologists, to perceive an accurate image of moving objects more than 50 feet away.

Male mayflies attract females in the waning hours of their brief adult lives by a swarming nuptial dance, shown here against the backdrop of a Florida sunset. As mature insects, mayflies have time for little but mating, for at that stage their life-span averages only a few hours (the name of their order, Ephemeroptera, stems from a Greek word that means "living a day"). Mayfly nymphs undergo an unusual preliminary stage before becoming true adults. When the nymph leaves its underwater world it is a pale-looking winged creature called a subimago that no longer breathes through gills and can at once flutter to the shore. But before it becomes a mature mayfly, it must undergo one last molt, finally emerging as a glistening adult mayfly. It is this final molting of a creature already equipped with functional wings that is unique among insects.

47

Grasshoppers and Their Kin

The orders of insects that include grasshoppers, cockroaches, praying mantises, termites and walking sticks and their kin share three highly important characteristics. First, they evolved in the same geological period, about 300 million years ago, and are thus among the oldest forms of insect life. Second, each undergoes an incomplete metamorphosis, never displaying the radical changes of the pupal stage. Third, all have the same wing structure. A newly hatched grasshopper, roach or termite nymph can easily be recognized as a tiny image of its parents—unlike the larvae of more advanced insects, which usually look nothing at all like their forebears until they emerge from their pupal cocoons or shells. In nearly every other trait of behavior and appearance, grasshoppers, crickets, katydids and locusts, cockroaches, mantises, walking sticks, leaf imitators (Orthoptera) and termites (Isoptera) are about as different from one another as any groups of insects.

The orthopteroids, for example, are set apart as the master masqueraders among the insects. The walking sticks look enough like twigs to fool any predator. They remain apparently motionless during the day and move slowly about in search of vegetation under cover of darkness. Their relatives, the leaf insects, are equally remarkable in their disguise as bogus leaves, which has convinced natives of tropical lands that these animals actually began life as buds on trees or bushes. Neither the stick nor leaf insects will drop their disguise under duress; even when handled, they usually remain motionless.

Certain tropical mantises, too, are clever mimics, posing in flowerbeds and nodding their brightly colored heads in the breeze, in unison with real flowers, until some insect approaches. Indeed, "preying" mantids might be a better name for the oddly constructed praying mantises, for they are rapacious killers that are esteemed by many farmers for consumption of crop-destroying insects.

Some representatives of Orthoptera—the grasshoppers, crickets and katydids—are notorious for their destructiveness. Ever since man began depending on crops for food, their depredations on agriculture have left famine and misery in their wake. They are also the noisy string sections of the insect orchestra. The music often carries an amorous message. The male katydid, for instance, raises an upper wing like a violin bow, draws it over a filelike ridge on the other wing and, by means of a tiny chitinous amplifier, transmits a trysting call to females that they can hear a mile away.

Among the great scourges of the earth, the swarms of locusts that periodically ravage great areas of orchards and farmlands are actually a kind of short-horned grasshopper, usually relatively harmless loners that are found in deserts and semideserts. But at irregular intervals a long period of dry weather forces the grasshopper-locust population to crowd together for moisture and food; their overcrowded habitat can no longer support them. Then they undergo a Jekyll–Hyde change. Their wings grow longer and they swarm together and take to the skies in search of food. "A fire devoureth before them," mourns the Bible's Book of Joel, "and behind them a flame burneth: the land is as the Garden of Eden before them, and behind them a desolate wilderness; yea, and nothing shall escape them." One swarm, 100 feet thick and a mile wide, flying at six miles per hour, took nine hours to pass an observer.

The colonies of tropical termites represent an equally impressive but radically different type of insect gathering. Termites congregate in masses that may number in the millions, carrying on a societal life older than any other on earth. Their mammoth adobe castles, sometimes a yard thick, 10 feet in diameter and a dozen feet high, are miracles of insectile architecture.

Termite colonies have been known to last 50 years or longer. Always at the core of the termitarium, and of the colony's life, is a fat queen that lays 8,000 to 10,000 eggs a day. The queen often lives as long as the colony itself. Should some disaster befall her, though, a hormonal inhibitor that normally causes nymphs to develop into sterile workers and soldiers is mysteriously relaxed. In a couple of weeks one of the nymphs will become the new queen.

Although all termites do not devour wood, many do, despite the odd fact that they are not innately equipped to digest it. In order to break down and absorb the tough cellulose fibers of wood, the termite most feared by homeowners harbors its own colony of protozoa, one-celled creatures that change the chemical composition of the wood so that it can be digested. The protozoa are fed to the nymphs by workers. The wood-eating cockroaches, too, have worked out a relationship with protozoans that live in their digestive systems. One species of roach has even managed to stake out its very own niche in the urban ecosystem—holing up in the cozy, warm interiors of television sets and eating the insulation off the wiring.

48

Wedding Feast

The most conspicuous members of the order Orthoptera, mantids are voracious predators of beetles, wasps, cockroaches and caterpillars. But female mantises also have a keen appetite for the male of the species, which becomes a more accessible victim at mating time in late summer. Then, as in the photograph above, a male may find his mate eating his head in the midst of reproducing. Decapitated, dismembered or not, the male still manages to complete the act before dying.

This connubial cannibalism is nature's efficient way of providing sustenance for the eggs that the female will lay, especially in cool climates where fall curtails her normal ration of live insects. In the late fall she secures her eggs to a twig or stem. Then she dies, and the eggs develop in their tough, weatherproof case over the winter. In the spring, from 50 to 300 tiny mantids emerge (right), molting immediately and leaving tassels of cast-off skins hanging from the abandoned egg case.

Unlikely-looking Relatives

Leaf insects, like the walking stick above, are masters of rigidity, capable of remaining motionless for hours on end, a characteristic known as thanatosis. Walking sticks abound in tropical rain forests, where they move about feeding at night and hang with almost no detectable movement by day. It is among walking sticks that one finds the longest insect on record—a remarkable 13 inches.

Among their more active kin, many katydids (opposite, above) and grasshoppers have slender bodies colored with greens and browns that blend in well with the grass stems, twigs and leaves where they live. Not so with the outlandish "sunset" grasshopper of Madagascar (opposite, below), whose gaudy color scheme is a signal to would-be predators that it is distasteful.

52

A katydid nymph (left), whose wings have not yet matured, perches on a flower. When the wings grow, musical instruments called organs of stridulation will develop on the wing covers—a file on one and a scraper on the other. These are rasped together—as many as 50 million times in a single summer—and amplified by the wing membranes, broadcasting the tireless katydid's familiar "Katy-did, katy-didn't" song in a summer evening's insect symphony.

The Locusts Are Coming

When their food supply is ample and climatic conditions are favorable for breeding during several successive years, normally solitary short-horned grasshoppers may reproduce to such a degree that overcrowding drives multitudes of them on a path of destruction. Beginning their trek as wingless nymphs, the insects surge across the landscape on foot, developing extra-long wings as they travel and finally taking to the air (right), where they sometimes blot out the horizon. Such ravenous plagues of migratory grasshoppers, or locusts, settle downward and devour any vegetation they encounter (above), sometimes maintaining a daily food consumption estimated to be equivalent to that of 1.5 million people.

archy declares war

by Don Marquis

For more than 60 years archy, the cockroach with the soul of a poet, has had a lasting place in the affections of the reading public. archy's first poem appeared in the New York Sun *in 1916 in the column of his creator, newsman Don Marquis. Each night after the* Sun's *last edition had gone to press, the cockroach bard crawled out and expressed himself on Marquis' typewriter by hurling his tiny body on each key. Since he was unable to manage capital letters or do much about punctuation marks, his singular lower-case style is unmistakable. His cockroach call to arms,* archy declares war, *is reprinted below, with illustrations by George Herriman, a contemporary of Marquis' and creator of the classic comic-strip character, Krazy Kat.*

i am going to start
a revolution
i saw a kitchen
worker killing
water bugs with poison
hunting pretty
little roaches
down to death
it set my blood to
boiling
i thought of all
the massacres and slaughter
of persecuted insects
at the hands of cruel humans

and i cried
aloud to heaven
and i knelt
on all six legs
and vowed a vow
of vengeance
i shall organize the insects
i shall drill them
i shall lead them
i shall fling a billion
times a billion billion
risen insects in an army
at the throats
of all you humans
unless you sign the papers
for a damn site better treatment
volunteers volunteers
hearken to my calling
fifty million flies
are wanted may the first
to die in marmalade
curses curses curses
on the cruel human race
does not the poor mosquito
love her little offspring
that you swat against the wall
out of equatorial
swamps and fever jungles
come o mosquitoes
a billion billion strong
and sting a billion baldheads
till they butt against each other
and break like egg shells
caterpillars locusts
grasshoppers gnats
vampire moths
black legged spiders
with red hearts of hell
centipedes and scorpions
little gingery ants

come come come
come you tarantulas
with fury in your feet
bloodsuckers wriggle
out of the bayous
ticks cooties hornets
give up your pleasures
all your little trivial
sunday school picnics
this is war
in earnest
and red revolution
come in a cloud
with a sun hiding miracle
of small deadly wings
swarm stab and bite
what we want is justice
curses curses curses
over land air and water
whirl in a million
sweeping and swaying
cyclonic dances

whirl high and swoop
down on the cities
like a comet bearing death
in the loop and flick
of its tail
little little creatures
out of all your billions
make great dragons
that lie along the sky
and war with the sunset
and eat up the moon
draw all the poison
from the evil stars
and spit it on the earth
remember every planet
pivots on an atom
and so you are strong
i swear by the great
horned toad of mithridates
i swear by the vision
of whiskered old pythagoras
that i am very angry
i am mad as hell
for i have seen a soapy
kitchen mechanic
murdering my brothers
slaying little roaches
pathetic in their innocence
damn her red elbows
damn her spotted apron
damn her steamy hair
damn her dull eyes
that look like a pair
of little pickled onions
curses curses curses
i even heard her praised
for undertaking murder
on her own volition
and called the only perfect
cook in the city

come come come
come in your billions
tiny small feet
and humming little wings
crawlers and creepers
wigglers and stingers
scratchers borers slitherers
little forked tongues
man is at your mercy
one sudden gesture
and all his empires perish
rise
strike for freedom
curses on the species
that invented roach poison
curses on the stingy
beings that evolved
tight zinc covers
that you can t crawl under
for their garbage cans
come like a sandstorm
spewed from the mouth
of a great apocalyptic
desert making devil
come like the spray
sooty and fiery
snorted from the nostrils
of a sky eating ogre
let us have a little
direct action is the
sincere wish of

archy

The Bugs

Only some of the insects among all those creeping, crawling, skittering creatures popularly referred to as bugs are actually true bugs. In fact, the term is reserved by entomologists for a single order of insects, the Heteroptera. In order to qualify as a bug, an insect must have two sets of wings that differ markedly from each other in their texture. The foremost pair of wings is thick where they join the body, gradually tapering and thinning to membranes at their ends; the hind pair, covered by the first set, are membranous throughout.

Bugs and the closely related winged insects, Homoptera, are what biologists call haustellate groups, a name stemming from the Latin verb *haustellare*, meaning "to drink"—which is a precise description of what bugs and their near kin do, using their mouth parts to pierce and then suck fluids from prey or vegetation. Their diet includes some of man's most valuable crops and domestic animals and sometimes man himself.

Among the most notorious of the true bugs are the bedbugs. They are hardy and can survive for as long as a year without a meal if they must, waiting patiently for some warm-blooded host to come along. Although bedbugs' bites are often painful, the bite of a near relative, the kissing bug, can be excruciating. In Latin America they are carriers of an often fatal disease called chagas.

The giant water bug, which grows to be more than four inches long in Latin America and India, hunts tadpoles and small fish, maneuvering its front legs like miniature nutcrackers to clasp its prey while the bug's sharp beak moves in to kill. Giant water bugs are a common Oriental food, and water boatmen, a related species found in ponds from Death Valley to the 15,000-foot timberline of the Himalayas, have long been cultivated in Egypt and Mexico for food. Stinkbugs, so called for the reeking secretions they leave on the fruits and berries they eat, are also considered a delicacy in some parts of the world.

The Homoptera—cicadas, leafhoppers, froghoppers, planthoppers, treehoppers, whiteflies, scale insects, aphids and plant lice—cause severe damage in gardens, farm fields and orchards. One species of cicada spends as long as 17 nymphal years underground, feeding on the roots of plants, until they emerge, usually in swarms, to take to the trees as the so-called "17-year locusts." The males, with their resonating musical organs, raise a mighty serenade for a few hours, then they mate with the females and thereupon die. The females outlive them only long enough to lay eggs but often long enough to do considerable damage to leaves and twigs of fruit trees before they, too, die, leaving the world for 16 silent springs before a new, noisy generation arises from the earth.

Sucking on a leaf in a head-down position, a froghopper nymph ingests so much sap so fast that the material must pass quickly through the creature's system, literally pouring out its anus. The digested sap flows down over the insect and is mixed with sticky material from glands on the abdomen. Appendages at the rear end whip the fluid into a frothy blob, and the insect lives inside this mass of spittle.

Scale insects, some of the most destructive parasites of trees and shrubs, manufacture another sort of covering for themselves, secreting a waxy or resinous overcoat that acts as armor plate against enemies and even protects the animal from insecticides.

Although many of the Homoptera are tiny creatures—some lace bugs are only two to five millimeters long—their capacity to cause damage results from the vast numbers of troops they can muster quickly into the field. If left undisturbed by such controls as ladybird beetles or by pesticides, the offspring of a lone female leafhopper could number some 500 million in a single year, and the generations spawned by one tiny aphid after less than a year could amount to 210 raised to the 15th power.

Contributing to the aphids' fertility is their curious ability to alternate normal sexual reproduction—the mating of males and females and the laying of eggs—with an unusual reproductive process called parthenogenesis. Wingless females give birth, without benefit of fertilization by a male, to still other wingless females. These in turn give parthenogenetic birth to another generation of winged females that usually migrate to a different plant from that on which their virgin grandmothers were originally hatched and there deliver yet another generation of live, wingless, fatherless female offspring. After several further cycles of parthenogenesis, live-born winged females eventually mate with sibling winged males and lay eggs to complete the circle. Both reproductive styles help ensure survival. Among aphids that live in temperate climates, the eggs are laid in the fall and are able to survive the winter. The parthenogenetic phases, beginning after eggs hatch in early spring, hasten an explosion of the aphid populations, insurance against the threats of predators.

Rhododendron leafhopper

Bugaboos

Man would be hard pressed to find a friend in the extraordinary rogue's gallery of bugs pictured on these pages. Even the relatively innocuous giant water bug (a male is shown opposite in his role as carrier of his mate's eggs) is nevertheless capable of delivering a painful bite. Leafhoppers like the red-and-green-banded common American species shown below the water bug cause millions of dollars of crop damage by introducing plant viruses or by sucking out juices.

The four-lined plant bug and the treehoppers, which comprise many thousands of species worldwide, resemble leafhoppers in subsisting primarily on the juices of plants, including crops. Treehoppers take many grotesque shapes, often with a greatly enlarged upper thorax that may resemble a thorn, an appearance that inspired the common name of one species shown here: thorn bugs. Wheel bugs are a particularly large species of assassin bug. The name "assassin" derives not only from their ability to inflict excruciating bites on humans and to transmit diseases but also from their habit of lying in ambush in flowers and plants to waylay bees and other unsuspecting insects that may alight nearby.

Treehopper

Plant bug

Giant water bug

Wheel bug (assassin bug)

Banded leafhopper

Treehopper (thorn bug)

61

Flies and Fleas

Among flies and fleas, members respectively of the orders Diptera and Siphonaptera, are many that are the greatest scourges of mankind. In the space of 20 years in the 14th century, the bubonic plague, carried by the rat flea, wiped out three quarters of the population of Europe and Asia. According to some experts, the mosquitoes that spread malaria and yellow fever have accounted, indirectly, for the deaths of about half of all human beings.

Fleas and flies are alike in having a complete metamorphosis, and, as larvae, they both have legless, simple bodies, all fat and digestive system. As adults, however, they are markedly different from each other. The bodies of fleas are vertically flat, an asset in slithering between the hairs of their hosts (usually mammals); their skin is hard enough to furnish protection from the nails and teeth of their victims. Fleas are wingless, but they have powerful legs that can propel them in leaps many times their own length. Flies are distinguished by a single pair of functional wings positioned in front. The hind wings have evolved into clubbed stems called halteres, which serve as organs of navigation; oscillating rapidly, the halteres are sensitive to changes in the fly's orientation.

Though fleas are without exception pestiferous—at any rate tormentors—one family of flies is of great value to man, and some others can be cited as having redeeming qualities. As larvae, tachinid flies live inside the bodies of other insects, among them the caterpillars of certain moths such as the gypsy and the brown tail, which are notorious destroyers of forests. The biteless true midge—as distinguished from the biting midge, or punkie—is blessedly incapable of feeding on people as an adult; as a larva, living in the water, it contributes enormously to the well-being of freshwater fish, which eat the midge larvae and other aquatic insects that also feed on midges. The blow fly, whose larvae are so strongly attracted to dead animal tissue that people once thought that putrefying meat spontaneously generated maggots, had a curious value to surgeons as late as World War I and is still in limited use. Placed in infected wounds, blow fly maggots swiftly clean them out—a function now almost entirely fulfilled by antibiotic drugs.

A great many other flies are, in one way or another, dangerous or annoying to man and other animals. Warble flies' larvae penetrate the skin of any creature they may encounter, usually cattle, and feed on the living flesh of their hosts. Animal victims sometimes die as a result, and there have been recorded instances of humans who succumbed to infestations of these so-called "macaque worms." Some flies have developed infinitely specialized roles for themselves, one subsisting solely on the feet of elephants, another on the scrotum of a particular North American squirrel. The ordinary housefly, summer intruder in nearly every home, carries with it some 33 million microorganisms in its gut and a half-billion more on its body and legs. Because it must expel some saliva while eating as part of its digestive processes, it necessarily leaves some of those organisms behind when it departs—millions of bacteria, which may include those of typhoid, tuberculosis and some 30 other diseases.

Among the 85,000 species of this fourth-largest order of insects, there are some Diptera that, although not necessarily transmitters of a dread disease, nonetheless inflict excruciating pain. The "no-seeum" of New England, a type of biting midge, is one example, as is the black fly of Canada, which harasses fishermen and has even been known to kill large cattle.

Diptera infest vegetation as well as animals. Among the plant parasites are cherry maggots, leaf miners, fruit flies and gall gnats, which cause the formation of cystlike galls on the stems of plants where the larvae live and wreak tremendous agricultural damage.

Faced with animals that are so hostile to him, man has retaliated. His efforts to control these insects have inevitably become both extremely important and highly controversial. Chemical pesticides such as DDT have been found gravely wanting. They affect beneficial insects and other animals harmfully and pollute water and soil. An equally grave concern is the fact that insects such as mosquitoes have counterattacked by developing strains that are immune to the chemicals.

The controls that do work are basic—such as draining marshes to eliminate aquatic mosquito larvae and carefully razoring or combing the eggs of parasitic botflies from the coats of horses. Recent research efforts, however, have opened a promising new avenue of control: the use of insect hormones duplicated in the laboratory. Scientists hope they will be able to destroy whole generations of pests, using chemicals that are specifically designed to destroy harmful species of insects. It is hoped that these compounds, properly formulated and prudently employed, will not likely affect any other living thing or change the environment in ways that would interfere with man's uses of soil and water.

Tachinid fly

Fruit fly

Snipe fly

Hessian fly

Lords of the Flies

Flies are a large and remarkably durable order, and, as this portrait gallery suggests, they differ widely in appearance, from the whiskery pursuer of flying insects, the robber fly, to the coral-colored fruit fly and the stalk-eyed flies of Africa, which might be fugitives from a science-fiction novel.

Though some flies serve mankind well, their usefulness is often outweighed by the harm they do. The ubiquitous fruit fly is an invaluable laboratory insect, one of the key experimental subjects in the study of genetics. Others also seem to be entirely beneficial. As an adult, the nectar-sipping bee fly is a useful pollinator of flowers. Its larva is a parasite that lives on caterpillars and is therefore regarded as a savior of woodlands and a good friend of foresters.

Most members of the order, though, are in a continuing state of war with man, and over the years the battle lines are sometimes extended almost accidentally. The Hessian fly, a gall midge (center row, left), crossed the Atlantic as a stowaway in the straw pallets of Hessian soldiers in the American Revolution—and became a major destroyer of grain crops.

64

Horsefly

Bee fly

Robber fly

Yellow dung fly

Stalk-eyed flies

Flower fly

Bluebottle fly

Mosquito's Ark

The bristling structure jutting out of the water at left is actually the image, much enlarged, of an intricate incubator, made up of 200 to 400 cylindrical mosquito eggs, floating as a quarter-inch-long raft. The minuscule ark is the creation of *Culex pipiens*, the familiar northern house mosquito. Only the female culex bites, and a meal of warm blood is an essential prelude to egg-laying. Without it the mother culex will lay no more than 40 to 50 eggs, which will not mature.

After hatching, the larvae drop from the raft into the water, where they develop just under the surface for seven days. As lumpy, active pupae they remain in the water. The final transformation from pupa to long-legged, glossy-winged mosquito takes place in just three to five minutes —one of the more incredibly quick changes in nature.

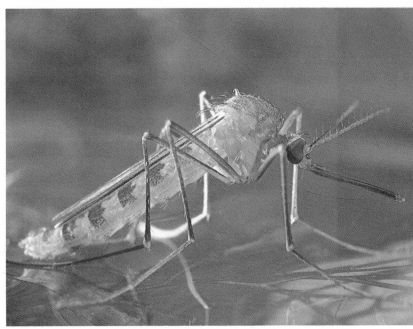

A newly fledged maiden mosquito pauses briefly on the surface of the water where she was spawned before taking to the air. Soon she will mate with one of the males of her generation—which all die during the autumn—and will carry her inseminated eggs through the winter, to lay them the following spring in any convenient body of water, from a puddle to a swamp.

Beetles

For their dazzlingly variegated color and baroque ornamentation, for the remarkable efficiency of their bodily structure, few creatures can match Coleoptera, the humble and often magnificent beetles. Their principal distinction from other insects is unique chitinous wing sheaths, the elytra, which they lift upward to release their operative wings when they take to the air. Beetles live all over the earth, in almost every kind of habitable environment. Many spend at least part of their lives underground or under the waters of streams and ponds.

Though some beetles are plain black, the order's attention-getters display gaudy colors. In shape, many suggest miniature rhinoceroses, elephants and giraffes. Some are iridescent, shimmering as they move. Others glow in the dark, and some of the more spectacular species can even flash in syncopated unison with their kin, whole trees full of male fireflies signaling prospective mates, pulsing together as precisely as an electronic billboard. (Some treacherous female fireflies of the genus *Photuris* blink beguilingly back at alien males, mimicking the light pulsations of alien females so accurately that the males flock to them—only to be eaten on arrival.)

The light-signal trap is merely one item in an inventory of beetle survival stratagems that is as numerous and variegated as the creatures themselves. (The order of beetles may number as many as a staggering quarter of a million species, almost five times as many as all vertebrate species.) Beetles range in size from the nearly microscopic *Trichopterygidae*, which measure just a hundredth of an inch in length, to giants like Macrocinus, whose legs alone are eight inches long, or *Dynastes hercules*, with a body four and a half inches in length.

Beetles are believed to have evolved from neuropteroids, daintily winged creatures such as lacewings, more than 300 million years ago. They have been remarkably successful since, maintaining their prehistoric skills and developing new ones. There are beetles that roll fresh dung into balls and bury them, submerging themselves—and perhaps a chum—for a feast. Others live in caves and cannibalize the corpses of fallen comrades. Still others specialize in the desiccated remains of spider prey, and there is an entire family of beetles that works busily as undertakers, interring whole snakes, frogs, moles and birds, sometimes burying them as deep as two feet below ground level to be reserved, like a dog's bone, for a later meal. One beetle, the lead cable borer, is so called because it is capable of munching its way through the lead sheathing on phone cables. Another, a flour beetle known scientifically, if somewhat mysteriously, as *Tribolium confusum*, is capable of eating its own weight in grain in a week. Aggrieved grain-elevator operators in the Great Plains regions estimate the confused flour beetle destroys as much as 10 percent of every harvest.

Like many other insects, some species of beetles at different stages in the metamorphic progression eat different foods. Thus, for example, the adult tiger beetle, in its quest for flying insect prey, does not compete for food with its larva, which eats earthbound ants and other beetles.

Beetles have been as versatile in developing defensive equipment as they have in evolving their modes of sustenance. In some cases, defenses consist in unpleasant toxic liquids. The searcher beetle, so called because it climbs high into trees in search of caterpillars, sprays a searing acid so potent it can raise blisters on human skin. The bombardier beetle literally fires its defensive fluid at would-be predators, driving off large ants or even reptiles and birds with artillery salvos of as many as 29 bursts in four minutes. The bombardier gets its firepower from a mechanism comprising two chambers. One is a reservoir where it separately stores three chemicals. When the bombardier opens a valve allowing these compounds to flow together into the third chamber, they form a pungent acid and react violently, spurting out through an orifice in the bombardier's body and driving would-be predators away.

Backing up such exotic defenses is the basic armament of all beetles—their hard, tough bodies. Their exoskeletons are so strong, in some cases, that they can sustain loads 800 to 1,700 times the weight of the beetle.

Though some Coleoptera are notoriously harmful—for instance, the Japanese beetle, an introduced species that has created havoc in gardens and on farms in the American Northeast—most perform useful and unsung services for man, indirectly as scavengers, by burying disease-breeding debris, aiding in the decomposition of waste and dead organisms, and directly as well. Ladybirds are a prime example, consuming huge populations of aphids and scale insects and making it possible for the California citrus industry to withstand the depredations of some of the most destructive agricultural pests. Ladybirds—the familiar polka-dotted "ladybugs"—are so useful economically, in fact, that they are sold commercially by the bagful to gardeners and orchardmen.

Great stag beetle

Adaptive Fancy Dress

The tortoise beetle has developed some unique devices to protect itself during each stage of its metamorphosis. The three tortoise beetle larvae above have undergone their first molt. But instead of discarding their dried skins like most molting insects, the grubs collect them on a kind of fork at the end of their tail, piling up skins from successive molts and forming a fancy-dress umbrella that may serve as camouflage to protect them from such predators as parasitic wasps.

As the beetles enter their pupal stage, the mass of dead skin is finally discarded. Although during this time the pupae hang motionless within their mummylike cases from the undersides of leaves, they undergo dramatic internal changes that result in a shimmering iridescent adult form (opposite). As adults, tortoise beetles resort to a different defense tactic. When threatened, they drop to the ground, where they play dead, feet in the air, until the danger has passed.

Seen from above in this photograph, the shimmering beauty of a tortoise beetle's upper surface makes it stand out against its leafy background. In nature their varied hues blend in with the many color gradations of their surroundings.

Its rounded wing sheaths resembling the arched carapace of its reptilian namesake, a tortoise beetle lays a packet of eggs. Some female tortoise beetles are very protective mothers, often clustering their eggs on leaf stalks, where they sit on the eggs until the larvae are hatched.

Baubles, Bangles and Beetles

Their gemlike colors and extraordinary shapes have marked beetles as insect collectors' items second only to butterflies and moths. One such prize is the North American dogbane beetle (above), whose shimmering metallic body looks like the work of a master goldsmith. Another is the silver-striped juniper beetle, an inhabitant of Mexico and the southwestern United States, a close relative of another famous jewel in the insectile crown, the sacred scarab of ancient Egypt.

Among other collectors' items is the four-eyed milkweed beetle, whose red-and-black shell warns predators that it has a bitter taste. The Japanese beetle's dramatic good looks do not offset its reputation as the alien scourge of American orchards, lawns and gardens. Found all over the world, the flat bark beetle usually hides its shell under the bark of trees, where it lives, feeds and breeds.

Silver-striped juniper beetle

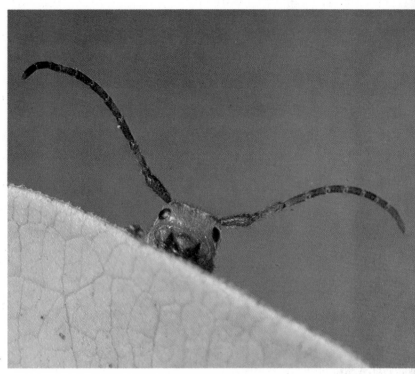

Four-eyed milkweed beetle

Japanese beetle

Flat bark beetle

73

The Sacred Beetle
by Jean Henri Fabre

The idea of a dung beetle—even the sacred scarab of ancient Egypt—fashioning a ball of cow excrement and rolling it away to its lair hardly sounds like the plot line of an absorbing story. Yet, when Fabre, the French entomologist and fabulist (pages 36–39), scrutinizes the humble beetle and its Sisyphean struggles under his magnifying glass, the event becomes high drama.

What excitement over a single patch of Cow-dung! Never did adventurers hurrying from the four corners of the earth display such eagerness in working a Californian claim. Before the sun becomes too hot, they are there in their hundreds, large and small, of every sort, shape and size, hastening to carve themselves a slice of the common cake. There are some that labour in the open air and scrape the surface; there are others that dig themselves galleries in the thick of the heap, in search of choice veins; some work the lower stratum and bury their spoil without delay in the ground just below; others again, the smallest, keep on one side and crumble a morsel that has slipped their way during the mighty excavations of their more powerful fellows. Some, newcomers and doubtless the hungriest, consume their meal on the spot; but the greater number dream of accumulating stocks that will allow them to spend long days in affluence, down in some safe retreat. A nice, fresh patch of dung is not found just when you want it, in the barren plains overgrown with thyme; a windfall of this sort is as manna from the sky; only fortunes' favourites receive so fair a portion. Wherefore the riches of to-day are prudently hoarded for the morrow. The stercoraceous scent has carried the glad tidings half a mile around; and all have hastened up to get a store of provisions. A few laggards are still arriving, on the wing or on foot.

Who is this that comes trotting towards the heap, fearing lest he reach it too late? His long legs move with awkward jerks, as though driven by some mechanism within his belly; his little red antennae unfurl their fan, a sign of anxious greed. He is coming, he has come, not without sending a few banqueters sprawling. It is the Sacred Beetle, clad all in black, the biggest and most famous of our Dung-beetles. Behold him at table, beside his fellow-guests, each of whom is giving the last touches to his ball with the flat of his broad fore-legs or else enriching it with yet one more layer before retiring to enjoy the fruit of his labours in peace. Let us follow the construction of the famous ball in all its phases.

The cylpeus, or shield, that is the edge of the broad, flat head, is notched with six angular teeth arranged in a semicircle. This constitutes the tool for digging and cutting up, the rake that lifts and casts aside the unnutritious vegetable fibres, goes for something better, scrapes and collects it. A choice is thus made, for these connoisseurs differentiate between one thing and another, making a rough selection when the Beetle is occupied with his own provender, but an extremely scrupulous one when it is a matter of constructing the maternal ball, which has a central cavity in which the egg will hatch. Then every scrap of fibre is conscientiously rejected and only the stercoral quintessence is gathered as the material for building the inner layer of the cell. The young larva, on issuing from the egg, thus finds in the very walls of its lodging a food of special delicacy which strengthens its digestion and enables it afterwards to attack the coarse outer layers.

74

Where his own needs are concerned, the Beetle is less particular and contents himself with a very general sorting. The notched shield then does its scooping and digging, its casting aside and scraping together more or less at random. The fore-legs play a mighty part in the work. They are flat, bow-shaped, supplied with powerful nervures and armed on the outside with five strong teeth. If a vigorous effort be needed to remove an obstacle or to force a way through the thickest part of the heap, the Dung-beetle makes use of his elbows, that is to say, he flings his toothed legs to right and left and clears a semicircular space with an energetic sweep. Room once made, a different kind of work is found for these same limbs: they collect armfuls of the stuff raked together by the shield and push it under the insect's belly, between the four hinder legs. These are formed for the turner's trade. They are long and slender, especially the last pair, slightly bowed and finished with a very sharp claw. They are at once recognized as compasses, capable of embracing a globular body in their curved branches and of verifying and correcting its shape. Their function is, in fact, to fashion the ball. . . .

Under a hot sun, when time presses, one stands amazed at the turner's feverish activity. And so the work proceeds apace: what a moment ago was a tiny pellet is now a ball the size of a walnut; soon it will be the size of an apple. I have seen some gluttons manufacture a ball the size of a man's fist. This indeed means food in the larder for days to come!

The Beetle has his provisions. The next thing is to withdraw from the fray and transport the victuals to a suitable place. Here the Scarab's most striking characteristics begin to show themselves. Straightway he begins his journey; he clasps his sphere with his two long hind-legs, whose terminal claws, planted in the mass, serve as pivots; he obtains a purchase with the middle pair of legs; and, with his toothed forearms, pressing in turn upon the ground, to do duty as levers, he proceeds with his load, he himself moving backwards, body bent, head down and hind-quarters in the air. The rear legs, the principal factor in the mechanism, are in continual movement backwards and forwards, shifting the claws to change the axis of rotation, to keep the load balanced and to push it along by alternate thrusts to right and left. . . .

And now to work with a will! The thing moves, it begins to roll; we shall get there, though not without difficulty. Here is a first awkward place: the Beetle is wending his way athwart a slope and the heavy mass tends to follow the incline; the insect, however, for reasons best known to itself, prefers to cut across this natural road, a bold project which may be brought to naught by a false step or by a grain of sand that disturbs the balance of the load. The false step is made: down goes the ball to the bottom of the valley; and the insect, toppled over by the shock, is lying on its back, kicking. It is soon up again and hastens to harness itself once more to its load. The machine works better than ever. But look out, you dunderhead! Follow the dip of the valley: that will save labour and mishaps; the road is good and level; your ball will roll quite easily. Not a bit of it! The Beetle prepares once again to mount the slope that has already been his undoing. Perhaps it suits him to return to the heights. Against that I have nothing to say: the Scarab's judgment is better than mine as to the advisability of keeping to lofty regions; he can see farther than I can in these matters. But at least take this path, which will lead you up by a gentle incline! Certainly not! Let him find himself near some very steep slope, impossible to climb, and that is the very path which the obstinate fellow will choose. Now begins a Sisyphean labour. The ball, that enormous burden, is painfully hoisted, step by step, with infinite precautions, to a certain height, always backwards. We wonder by what miracle of statics a mass of this size can be kept upon the slope. Oh! An ill-advised movement frustrates all this toil: the ball rolls down, dragging the Beetle with it. Once more the heights are scaled and another fall is the sequel. The attempt is renewed, with greater skill this time at the difficult points; a wretched grass-root, the cause of the previous falls, is carefully got over. We are almost there; but steady now, steady! It is a dangerous ascent and the merest trifle may yet ruin everything. For see, a leg slips on a smooth bit of gravel! Down come ball and Beetle, all mixed up together. And the insect begins over again, with indefatigable obstinacy. Ten times, twenty times, he will attempt the hopeless ascent, until his persistence vanquishes all obstacles, or until, wisely recognizing the futility of his efforts, he adopts the level road.

Love Bugs

If a contest were held for "Most Lovable Insect," surely the brightly colored ladybug (left and below) and the luminescent firefly (opposite) would be top contenders. Besides being lovable, the ladybugs—also called ladybirds and ladybird beetles—are among the most useful insects. Of the more than 4,000 species, most feed exclusively and insatiably on aphids, greenflies and scale insects, the despair of farmers and scourges of their crops. One ladybug was known to have polished off 90 adult and 3,000 larval scale insects during its own larval development.

In contrast, most adult fireflies eat nothing at all. Their larvae, however, prey on such garden pests as slugs and snails. Both larvae and adults are capable of producing the luminous glow that brightens up summer evenings. The light is refined in specialized organs in adult fireflies' abdomens. There the enzyme luciferase is oxidized with the fat, luciferin. The result is a greenish glow that is unequaled for its coolness, producing only 1/80,000 of the heat radiated by a candle of equal brightness.

Thousands of ladybugs of the species appropriately named Hippodamia convergens (an individual is seen at right) gather on a post in Arizona, where they remain together during the fall and winter months. Many species of ladybugs exhibit an almost uncanny homing instinct, successive generations wintering year after year at the exact place their elders met.

Like so many Christmas ornaments, hundreds of fireflies light up a tree in Malaysia (left), where, as in neighboring Thailand and elsewhere, their nightly illuminations are major tourist attractions. During the day the elongated, flattened bodies of these insects (above) can be seen hiding among leaves and other foliage. At night, however, they begin blinking their lights. Sexually mature males and females send out rhythmic light patterns to one another that signal the identity of their species. This ensures that members of the same species find one another in order to mate.

Bees, Wasps and Ants

Bees and ants have captured the human imagination through their intricate, complex societies. Yet, though all ants are social animals, most bees, as well as the majority of wasps, are solitary. All three groups, along with sawflies, belong to the order Hymenoptera (meaning "membrane-winged"), the third-largest insect order.

Among those Hymenoptera that keep to themselves, the goal of adult females—the class is a pure matriarchy in which males have no other role but to fertilize females—is to lay an egg in a place that will furnish the larva with nourishment when it hatches. Stinging Hymenoptera accomplish this in two basic ways. Depending on species, she may seek out and paralyze such prey as spiders with the sting in her abdomen's rear end, drag the trophy to a shelter, lay an egg on it and seal up the shelter. Alternatively, a wasp may lay an egg on the body of an unwitting victim or drill a hole into the body of an insect host and leave the egg inside. There, once hatched, the larva eats the living flesh of the host—usually with lethal effect.

Since the first primitive sawflies emerged some 200 million years ago, evolution from solitary life to the highly developed social organization of the honeybee and the ant has been a lengthy, complicated process. Societal origins can probably be seen, however, in the response to lean times of certain wasps that are usually solitary. When food is scarce, the wasp will make certain of her brood's survival by feeding the larvae everyday instead of storing food for the entire larval development or leaving her offspring alone to find food for themselves. Such a rudimentary parental relationship is the basis of insect societies.

In this instance, however, the concern of the parent is not altruistic or motherly in the sense understood by humans. Even in the case of the wasp turned temporary nurturing mother, it may be only a response to an instinctive transaction between adult and young called trophyllaxis. Simply defined, trophyllaxis is an exchange of substances between feeder and fed. In the feeding process, for instance, the exchange operates when the larva, stimultated by the prospect of food offered by an adult, excretes a drop of liquid that the adult quickly consumes. Occasionally the adult may take a kind of advantage of this arrangement, accepting the liquid without "paying off" in food. Thus, the larva, receiving less nourishment than it needs, may grow to adulthood with undeveloped sex organs. The result is a sterile female.

Such undernourished females have evolved into the busy, specialized workers of the ant colony and the beehive, laboring in their thousands—as many as 40,000 honeybees may occupy a single hive—for the well-being of a queen and her offspring.

These insect societies may be regarded as extended families—or as a single organism composed of many members. This concept is brought vividly to life in the periodic—and devastating—migrations of a colony of army ants, moving as a single unit millions strong, in search of a new food supply. Another striking example is the behavior of leafcutter ants of Central and South America, which dwell in colonies that sprawl across as much as half an acre of land. The ants may excavate more than 1,000 chambers, making a subterranean village that penetrates as deep as 15 feet into the earth. To this settlement, along paths that measure five inches wide and 100 yards long, the ants bring leaves that become the growing medium for underground fungus farms where they raise their food. The colony divides the work: The smallest ants tend the fungus beds, the intermediate-sized members bring in the leaves and the largest soldier ants defend the colony against intruders. Each ant has its predestined, undeviating role. Any suggestion of individualistic behavior is beyond the pale of instinct.

Equally impressive in a very different way is the curious evolution and degeneration of another kind of social arrangement among ants. This occurs among Amazon ants of western Europe, whose colonies are cared for by small black slave ants called *Formica fusca*. Superb fighters, Amazons have evolved long, sickle-shaped jaws that are virtually useless for anything but combat, and they can barely feed themselves. Without their *fusca* slaves, captured in periodic raids, they would be helpless. The slaves build and enlarge the Amazon nest and feed the Amazons and their brood. There is no conscious idea of deserting or refusing to serve their masters. The scene, according to British entomologist O. W. Richards, is extraordinary: large groups of Amazon workers, ". . . much bigger and more formidable than their slaves, spending the whole day doing nothing but occasionally cleaning themselves and soliciting the slaves for food." As Richards goes on to say, however, the picture of mighty Amazon dominance is false. Having become overdependent on the *fusca*, the Amazons are headed for extinction.

Bumblebee

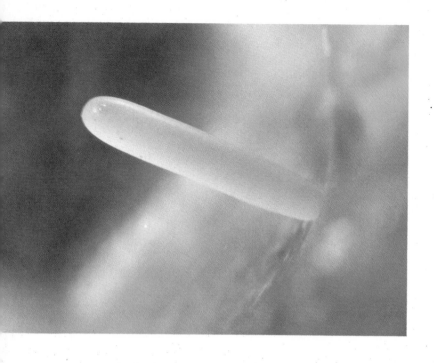

Bees' Beginnings

Honeybees have long been among man's favorite insects. Ancient Egyptian apiarists put tiered mud beehives on boats and drifted slowly down the Nile in search of waterfront blossoms. Greeks and Romans believed that the golden elixir bees produced was the food of the gods. This harvestable treasure is a product of the bees' seemingly ceaseless activities, which are directed mainly toward nurturing their young.

During summer, a queen bee lays upward of 3,000 eggs a day as she crawls over the comb searching out empty cells. She inserts her long abdomen into each cell and cements an egg, like the one shown greatly enlarged at left, to the bottom. Within four days the eggs hatch, and over the following days the larvae that emerge (below) increase in size over 1,500 times. On the sixth day the workers that have been caring for them cap the cells with wax. The bee young then enter the stage of pupation (opposite), which lasts about two weeks before the bees emerge as adults.

During the time when they are sealed in the cells, honeybee pupae gradually darken. The fully developed worker at the bottom of this cutaway view has shed its pupal skin and is almost ready to emerge by gnawing through the wax cap.

Before worker bees can begin their prime task of extracting nectar from blossoms (above) they spend the first three of their short five weeks of adult life in the hive, fulfilling a prolonged apprenticeship. Shortly after emerging from the cell (right), they are assigned routine hive-cleaning chores and are promoted successively to the duties of feeding the larvae and the queen, receiving food from field bees, secreting wax, repairing cells and guarding the hive.

The nectar that a forager brings back to the hive is passed back and forth between bees several times, a process that promotes chemical breakdown of the complex compound into a simple sugar. Then workers fan the nectar with their wings to evaporate the water, thus preventing fermentation and conserving storage space. For clarification, the process is shown here in a horizontal view, although in nature the workers pass and fan the nectar vertically along the comb.

The workers' most arduous task is satisfying the insatiable appetite of the newly hatched larvae. Each one of the future workers requires about 23 feedings a day.

The queen maintains her dominant position in the hive by means of a chemical that she secretes, which is passed on from worker to worker. When the "queen substance" grows weak because of the queen's age—or diluted because of the increasing population of the colony—workers begin to construct large, pendulous queen cells (right) where the larvae are fed extra-large portions of the protein-rich food called royal jelly in order to produce a new queen. If two queens should emerge from the royal cells at the same time, the rivals engage in a fight to the death (below) to establish control. Often the imminent birth of a new queen will prompt the old queen to depart and start a new hive, taking thousands of workers with her. One such swarm is shown on the opposite page, clinging to an apple tree while awaiting the reports of scouts on suitable new nesting sites.

Papermakers' Nests

The best-known wasp in temperate zones is the *Polistes* (opposite), whose paper nests are a common sight under the eaves of houses and garages. Despite the consternation these paper wasps create when they retreat indoors in late autumn to hibernate, they are relatively gentle and rarely sting except when provoked. They are also among the few wasps that form societies with workers, males and one or more queens, though the colonies they create are far more primitive than those of honeybees or ants.

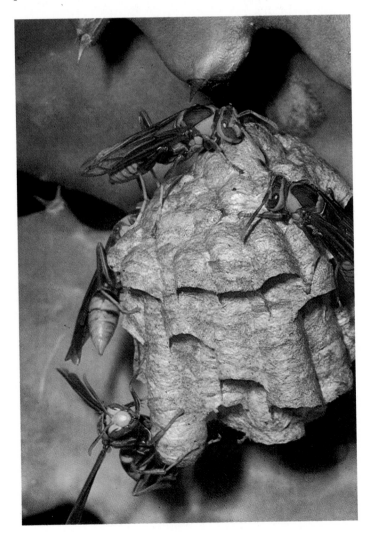

Like honeybees, wasps are relatively exacting architects. The fragile-looking paper nest of Polistes (left), fashioned from wood chewed into a kind of papier-mâché, is very strong, and the cells where eggs are laid are waterproofed to protect the emerging larvae from rain. The hanging nest above is constructed in faithful imitation of jungle leaves in Trinidad, its builder's habitat.

87

Mother Huntresses

Although most adult wasps feast only on fruit, nectar and other sugary treats, their larvae need protein to aid their growth and are usually carnivorous. As a result, many wasp mothers have become formidable hunters in their pursuit of other insects to provision the nursery larder. They tend to be finicky about what they feed their young, though, and instinctively prey on only one group—for example, cicadas, honeybees or certain caterpillars.

But the wasps rarely kill their victims. Their sting usually leaves prey paralyzed but alive so as to provide up to 40 days' fresh food for wasp larvae. Most hunters bury their catch in a burrow with their eggs, but the potter wasp (below) fashions a graceful clay vase before laying an egg inside and stocking it with caterpillars for the larvae.

Not all wasp victims are buried alive with eggs. The meadow grasshopper felled by a social wasp (right) is destined to be chewed up into a paste and fed to larvae hatched in open cells.

A cicada wasp, which takes her name from her prey, stuns a catch. She has a roundabout method of getting her heavy burden home. She drags the cicada up the nearest tree until she is high enough to take off and glide with her victim back to her burrow.

Eggs' Benefit

Rather than hauling oversized prey back to a nest, the often diminutive parasitic wasps use the bodies of other insects as a combination incubator and food store. The host is usually the larva of another species, such as the caterpillar at left. The tiny silken cocoons covering the pupae were spun by the well-fed larvae of the braconid wasp as they emerge from an egg implanted in its body by a female adult. Many other parasitic wasps have developed specialized ovipositors to inject their eggs directly into their prey. The spindly ichneumon female below is using her long black ovipositor to bore a hole in tree bark and reach the burrow of a horntail grub inside.

Mandibles: Ants' Basic Equipment

The mandibles of the ant, shown greatly magnified here, are powerful, specialized weapons and tools, far more diversified in these familiar insects than in their closest relatives, the bees and wasps. Some ants can deliver painful stings; most rely on their well-developed mandibles not only to subdue prey and attack intruders but also to excavate their mazelike tunnels.

Ants differ from other members of the order Hymenoptera —mostly skilled aviators—by being virtually landbound. Only the queen and a few short-lived males grow wings for use during the mating season, and the queen quickly disposes of hers after her nuptial flight, often tearing them off and eating them. Starting with the first few workers raised by a queen, nearly all ants build a highly stratified colonial society, with well-defined roles for workers as nursemaids, soldiers, foragers and sometimes gardeners.

The mandibles of the driver ant—shown thrusting at prey like a pair of scimitars—have made this ant one of the most dreaded creatures in the African jungle. A horde of advancing drivers has been known to reduce a penned cow to bare bones in a matter of hours.

Societies
of Specialists

Ants are not only among the most numerous of land animals but also among the most versatile. Their adaptability
is so great that it has convinced some observers that ants
can live almost anywhere and eat almost anything. The
driver ants shown at right, crossing an African stream on
a bridge of twigs, are meat-eating nomads that live off the
land and pause in their destructive trek through the jungle
only long enough for their queen to lay and hatch her eggs.

Strict vegetarians, the leafcutters (opposite, below) are
dedicated farmers, carefully cultivating underground fungus gardens.

Most ants live below ground, though many nest in trees
and other plants. An extraordinary nest-building adapta-
tion is displayed by the tree-dwelling Australian tent-
maker, which manufactures tight structures out of leaves
fastened together with silk. Since adult ants do not manufacture silk, they get it from mature larvae, which they
pick up and squeeze, causing them to secrete silk. Then the
adults use the silk to bind leaves together, just as a human
would pinch a dab of plastic cement out of a tube.

*Hauling a dead yellow jacket home, a
scavenger ant demonstrates its tenacity
as well as its remarkable strength. A
forager ant can carry up to 27 times her
own weight, using muscles adapted to
give her extra leverage for lifting,
pushing and dragging.*

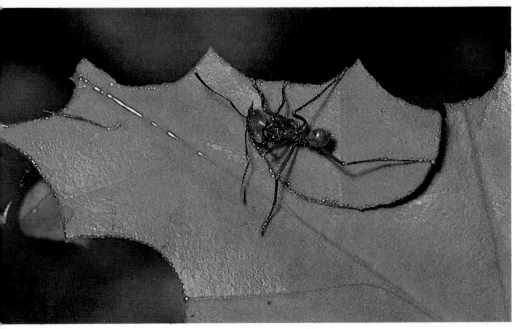

The South American leafcutter ant (left) uses the serrated edges of her asymmetrical mandibles like a pair of pinking shears when precisely snipping a disk of foliage. Plantation owners know leafcutters as serious pests that can defoliate valuable coffee or citrus trees virtually overnight.

Leiningen Versus the Ants

by Carl Stephenson

The horrifying spectacle of millions of army ants on the march, reducing every living creature in their path to rubble and bones, is a recurrent and grossly exaggerated nightmare of the South American heartland. In his chilling short story, "Leiningen Versus the Ants," excerpted here, Carl Stephenson tells of the grim confrontation of one man with such a fictional horde. After the invaders have destroyed the neighboring plantation, Leiningen, a prosperous planter, decides to defend his land and workers from a position behind two moats. The ants easily cross the first moat, and Leiningen prepares what is literally a last-ditch defense.

He rose with the sun and went out on the flat roof of his house. And a scene like one from Dante lay around him; for miles in every direction there was nothing but a black, glittering multitude, a multitude of rested, sated, but none the less voracious ants: yes, look as far as one might, one could see nothing but that rustling black throng, except in the north, where the great river drew a boundary they could not hope to pass. But even the high stone breakwater, along the bank of the river, which Leiningen

had built as a defence against inundations, was, like the paths, the shorn trees and shrubs, the ground itself, black with ants.

So their greed was not glutted in razing that vast plantation? Not by a long chalk; they were all the more eager now on a rich and certain booty—four hundred men, numerous horses, and bursting granaries.

At first it seemed that the petrol trench would serve its purpose. The besiegers sensed the peril of swimming it, and made no move to plunge blindly over its brink. Instead they devised a better maneuver; they began to collect shreds of bark, twigs and dried leaves and dropped these into the petrol. Everything green, which could have been similarly used, had long since been eaten. After a time, though, a long procession could be seen bringing from the west the tamarind leaves used as rafts the day before.

Since the petrol, unlike the water in the outer ditch, was perfectly still, the refuse stayed where it was thrown. It was several hours before the ants succeeded in covering an

appreciable part of the surface. At length, however, they were ready to proceed to a direct attack.

Their storm troops swarmed down the concrete side, scrambled over the supporting surface of twigs and leaves, and impelled these over the few remaining streaks of open petrol until they reached the other side. Then they began to climb up this to make straight for the helpless garrison.

During the entire offensive, the planter sat peacefully, watching them with interest, but not stirring a muscle. Moreover, he had ordered his men not to disturb in any way whatever the advancing horde. So they squatted listlessly along the bank of the ditch and waited for a sign from the boss.

The petrol was now covered with ants. A few had

97

climbed the inner concrete wall and were scurrying towards the defenders.

"Everyone back from the ditch!" roared Leiningen. The men rushed away, without the slightest idea of his plan. He stooped forward and cautiously dropped into the ditch a stone which split the floating carpet and its living freight, to reveal a gleaming patch of petrol. A match spurted, sank down to the oily surface—Leiningen sprang back; in a flash a towering rampart of fire encompassed the garrison.

This spectacular and instant repulse threw the Indians into ecstasy. They applauded, yelled and stamped, like children at a pantomime. Had it not been for the awe in which they held the boss, they would infallibly have carried him shoulder high.

It was some time before the petrol burned down to the bed of the ditch, and the wall of smoke and flame began to lower. The ants had retreated in a wide circle from the devastation, and innumerable charred fragments along the outer bank showed that the flames had spread from the holocaust in the ditch well into the ranks beyond, where they had wrought havoc far and wide.

Yet the perseverance of the ants was by no means broken; indeed, each setback seemed only to whet it. The concrete cooled, the flicker of the dying flames wavered and vanished, petrol from the second tank poured into the trench—and the ants marched forward anew to the attack.

The foregoing scene repeated itself in every detail, except that on this occasion less time was needed to bridge the ditch, for the petrol was now already filmed by a layer of ash. Once again they withdrew; once again petrol flowed into the ditch. Would the creatures never learn that their self-sacrifice was utterly senseless? It really was senseless, wasn't it? Yes, of course it was senseless—provided the defenders had an *unlimited* supply of petrol.

When Leiningen reached this stage of reasoning, he felt for the first time since the arrival of the ants that his confidence was deserting him. His skin began to creep; he loosened his collar. Once the devils were over the trench there·wasn't a chance in hell for him and his men. God,

what a prospect, to be eaten alive like that!

For the third time the flames immolated the attacking troops, and burned down to extinction. Yet the ants were coming on again as if nothing had happened. And meanwhile Leiningen had made a discovery that chilled him to the bone—petrol was no longer flowing into the ditch. Something must be blocking the outflow pipe of the third and last cistern—a snake or a dead rat? Whatever it was, the ants could be held off no longer, unless petrol could by some method be led from the cistern into the ditch.

Then Leiningen remembered that in an outhouse nearby were two old disused fire engines. Spry as never before in their lives, the peons dragged them out of the shed, connected their pumps to the cistern, uncoiled and laid the hose. They were just in time to aim a stream of petrol at a column of ants that had already crossed and drive them back down the incline into the ditch. Once more an oily girdle surrounded the garrison, once more it was possible to hold the position—for the moment.

It was obvious, however, that this last resource meant only the postponement of defeat and death. A few of the peons fell on their knees and began to pray; others, shrieking insanely, fired their revolvers at the black, advancing masses, as if they felt their despair was pitiful enough to sway fate itself to mercy.

At length, two of the men's nerves broke: Leiningen saw a naked Indian leap over the north side of the petrol trench, quickly followed by a second. They sprinted with incredible speed towards the river. But their fleetness did not save them; long before they could attain the rafts, the enemy covered their bodies from head to foot.

In the agony of their torment, both sprang blindly into the wide river, where enemies no less sinister awaited them. Wild screams of mortal anguish informed the breathless onlookers that crocodiles and sword-toothed piranhas were no less ravenous than ants, and even nimbler in reaching their prey.

In spite of this bloody warning, more and more men showed they were making up their minds to run the blockade. Anything, even a fight midstream against alligators, seemed better than powerlessly waiting for death to come and slowly consume their living bodies.

Leiningen flogged his brain till it reeled. Was there nothing on earth could sweep this devil's spawn back into the hell from which it came?

Then out of the inferno of his bewilderment rose a terrifying inspiration. Yes, one hope remained, and one alone. It might be possible to dam the great river completely, so that its waters would fill not only the water ditch but overflow into the entire gigantic "saucer" of land in which lay the plantation.

The far bank of the river was too high for the waters to escape that way. The stone breakwater ran between the river and the plantation; its only gaps occurred where the "horseshoe" ends of the water ditch passed into the river. So its waters would not only be forced to inundate into the plantation, they would also be held there by the breakwater until they rose to its own high level. In half an hour, perhaps even earlier, the plantation and its hostile army of occupation would be flooded.

The ranch house and outbuildings stood upon rising ground. Their foundations were higher than the break-

99

water, so the flood would not reach them. And any remaining ants trying to ascend the slope could be repulsed by petrol.

It was possible—yes, if one could only get to the dam! A distance of nearly two miles lay between the ranch house and the weir—two miles of ants. Those two peons had managed only a fifth of that distance at the cost of their lives. Was there an Indian daring enough after that to run the gauntlet five times as far? Hardly likely; and if there were, his prospect of getting back was almost nil.

No, there was only one thing for it, he'd have to make the attempt himself; he might just as well be running as sitting still, anyway, when the ants finally got him. Besides, there was a bit of a chance. Perhaps the ants weren't so almighty, after all; perhaps he had allowed the mass suggestion of that evil black throng to hypnotize him, just as a snake fascinates and overpowers.

The ants were building their bridges. Leiningen got up on a chair. "Hey, lads, listen to me!" he cried. Slowly and listlessly, from all sides of the trench, the men began to shuffle towards him, the apathy of death already stamped on their faces.

"Listen, lads!" he shouted. "You're frightened of those beggars, but you're a damn sight more frightened of me, and I'm proud of you. There's still a chance to save our lives—by flooding the plantation from the river. Now one of you might manage to get as far as the weir—but he'd never come back. Well, I'm not going to let you try it; if I did I'd be worse than one of those ants. No, I called the tune, and now I'm going to pay the piper.

"The moment I'm over the ditch, set fire to the petrol. That'll allow time for the flood to do the trick. Then all you have to do is wait here all snug and quiet till I'm back. Yes, I'm coming back, trust me"—he grinned—"when I've finished my slimming-cure."

He pulled on high leather boots, drew heavy gauntlets over his hands, and stuffed the spaces between the breeches and boots, gauntlets and arms, shirt and neck, with rags soaked in petrol. With close-fitting mosquito goggles he shielded his eyes, knowing too well the ants' dodge of first robbing their victim of sight. Finally, he plugged his nostrils and ears with cottonwool, and let the peons drench his clothes with petrol.

He was about to set off, when the old Indian medicine man came up to him; he had a wondrous salve, he said, prepared from a species of chafer whose odor was intolerable to ants. Yes, this odor protected these chafers from the attacks of even the most murderous ants. The Indian smeared the boss' boots, his gauntlets, and his face over and over with the extract.

Leiningen then remembered the paralyzing effect of ants' venom, and the Indian gave him a gourd full of the medicine he had administered to the bitten peon at the water ditch. The planter drank it down without noticing its bitter taste; his mind was already at the weir.

He started off towards the northwest corner of the trench. With a bound he was over—and among the ants.

The beleaguered garrison had no opportunity to watch Leiningen's race against death. The ants were climbing the inner bank again—the lurid ring of petrol blazed aloft. For the fourth time that day the reflection from the fire shone on the sweating faces of the imprisoned men, and on the reddish-black cuirasses of their oppressors. The red and blue, dark-edged flames leaped vividly now, celebrating what? The funeral pyre of the four hundred, or of the hosts of destruction?

Leiningen ran. He ran in long, equal strides, with only one thought, one sensation, in his being—he *must* get through. He dodged all trees and shrubs; except for the split seconds his soles touched the ground the ants should have no opportunity to alight on him. That they would get to him soon, despite the salve on his boots, the petrol in his clothes, he realized only too well, but he knew even more surely that he must, and that he would, get to the weir.

Apparently the salve was some use after all; not until he reached halfway did he feel ants under his clothes, and a few on his face. Mechanically, in his stride, he struck at them, scarcely conscious of their bites. He saw he was drawing appreciably nearer the weir—the distance grew less and less—sank to five hundred—three—two—one hundred yards.

Then he was at the weir and gripping the ant-hulled wheel. Hardly had he seized it when a horde of infuriated ants flowed over his hands, arms and shoulders. He started the wheel—before it turned once on its axis the swarm covered his face. Leiningen strained like a madman, his lips pressed tight; if he opened them to draw breath. . . .

He turned and turned; slowly the dam lowered until it reached the bed of the river. Already the water was overflowing the ditch. Another minute, and the river was pouring through the near-by gap in the breakwater. The flooding of the plantation had begun.

Leiningen let go the wheel. Now, for the first time, he realized he was coated from head to foot with a layer of ants. In spite of the petrol, his clothes were full of them, several had got to his body or were clinging to his face.

Now that he had completed his task, he felt the smart raging over his flesh from the bites of sawing and piercing insects.

Frantic with pain, he almost plunged into the river. To be ripped and splashed to shreds by piranhas? Already he was running the return journey, knocking ants from his gloves and jacket, brushing them from his bloodied face, squashing them to death under his clothes.

One of the creatures bit him just below the rim of his goggles; he managed to tear it away, but the agony of the bite and its etching acid drilled into the eye nerves; he saw now through circles of fire into a milky mist, then he ran for a time almost blinded, knowing that if he once tripped and fell. . . . The old Indian's brew didn't seem much good; it weakened the poison a bit, but didn't get rid of it. His heart pounded as if it would burst; blood roared in his ears; a giant's fist battered his lungs.

Then he could see again, but the burning girdle of petrol appeared infinitely far away; he could not last half that distance. Swift-changing pictures flashed through his head, episodes in his life, while in another part of his brain a cool and impartial onlooker informed this ant-blurred, gasping, exhausted bundle named Leiningen that such a rushing panorama of scenes from one's past is seen only in the moment before death.

A stone in the path . . . too weak to avoid it . . . the planter stumbled and collapsed. He tried to rise . . . he must be pinned under a rock . . . it was impossible . . . the slightest movement was impossible. . . .

Then all at once he saw, starkly clear and huge, and, right before his eyes, furred with ants, towering and swaying in its death agony, the pampas stag. In six minutes—gnawed to the bones. God, he *couldn't* die like that! And something outside him seemed to drag him to his feet. He tottered. He began to stagger forward again.

Through the blazing ring hurtled an apparition which, as soon as it reached the ground on the inner side, fell full length and did not move. Leiningen, at the moment he made that leap through the flames, lost consciousness for the first time in his life. As he lay there, with glazing eyes and lacerated face, he appeared a man returned from the grave. The peons rushed to him, stripped off his clothes, tore away the ants from a body that seemed almost one open wound; in some places the bones were showing. They carried him into the ranch house.

As the curtain of flames lowered, one could see in place of the illimitable host of ants an extensive vista of water. The thwarted river had swept over the plantation, carrying with it the entire army. The water had collected and mounted in the great "saucer," while the ants had in vain attempted to reach the hill on which stood the ranch house. The girdle of flames held them back.

And so imprisoned between water and fire, they had been delivered into the annihilation that was their god. And near the farther mouth of the water ditch, where the stone mole had its second gap, the ocean swept the lost battalions into the river, to vanish forever.

The ring of fire dwindled as the water mounted to the petrol trench, and quenched the dimming flames. The inundation rose higher and higher: because its outflow was impeded by the timber and underbrush it had carried along with it, its surface required some time to reach the top of the high stone breakwater and discharge over it the rest of the shattered army.

It swelled over ant-stippled shrubs and bushes, until it washed against the foot of the knoll whereon the besieged had taken refuge. For a while an alluvial of ants tried again and again to attain this dry land, only to be repulsed by streams of petrol back into the merciless flood.

Leiningen lay on his bed, his body swathed from head to foot in bandages. With fomentations and salves, they had managed to stop the bleeding, and had dressed his many wounds. Now they thronged around him, one question in every face. Would he recover? "He won't die," said the old man who had bandaged him, "if he doesn't want to."

The planter opened his eyes. "Everything in order?" he asked.

"They're gone," said his nurse. "To hell." He held out to his master a gourd full of a powerful sleeping draught. Leiningen gulped it down.

"I told you I'd come back," he murmured, "even if I am a bit streamlined." He grinned and shut his eyes. He slept.

Butterflies and Moths

Bright patches of airborne color, dancing under the sun in a summer meadow, butterflies are among the most compellingly beautiful of insects. Many a moth, too, rivals the most gorgeous butterflies in dazzling, tinted displays of patterned wings, which are covered by tiny scales splashed, in some species, with all the colors of the rainbow. (Lepidoptera, the name of the order to which butterflies and moths belong, means "scaled wings.") The order, comprising 140,000 species, is the largest group of insects except the beetles. Its members vary in size more than any other insect group, from the one-foot wingspan of one species of South American owlet moth to the quarter-inch span of a certain type of Eriocranid moth.

The number and variety of these creatures may account for the fact that even expert lepidopterists have trouble describing the differences between butterflies and moths. To every rough rule of thumb (moths fly at night, butterflies by day; moths have hairier, thicker bodies than butterflies) there are so many exceptions that succinct definitions are virtually impossible.

Like many insects, butterflies and moths both undergo complete metamorphosis. Few insects, however, can match—for sheer magic—the astonishing transformation that attends the final stages in the metamorphosis of the bright-hued species of Lepidoptera, when the caterpillar or larva first becomes a pupa and then emerges as an adult: winged, sexually mature, equipped with highly sophisticated organs of taste, smell and sometimes hearing to find food and seek out its mate.

To examine the steps leading to this magical transformation, an observer might begin by watching the caterpillar of the European swallowtail butterfly as it comes to rest on a vertical twig following an increasingly torpid, weary climb. Its body is responding to a command issued from a minute set of glands called the *corpora allata* that are found in all insects. These glands are the source of what biologists now recognize as an all-important "juvenile hormone," which maintains the creature in its larval stage as long as the substance is secreted.

When production of the juvenile hormone stops, hormones of a different sort continue to be secreted. Pupal life—the intermediary stage between caterpillar and adult butterfly—begins. At this time the caterpillar sheds its bright-colored skin to reveal the drab shroud of its chrysalis, where it will pupate. Within the chrysalis, which still vaguely bears the segmented outline of its larval incarnation, the creature seems outwardly dead, a motionless husk.

Motionless—but far from dead. Inside the chrysalis powerful life forces are at work. The larval cells of the caterpillar are indeed dying, a process triggered by the cutoff of juvenile hormone, but in their place adult cells that have lain dormant within the caterpillar's body are now beginning to develop. Slowly or rapidly, over a period that may range from 10 days to seven months, depending on the season, these cells grow and rearrange themselves into the altogether new creature that will emerge from the chrysalis as an adult.

This infinitely complex change has a clear-cut biological function: Larvae and adults are enabled to pursue separate modes of life that are ideally suited to their vastly different functions and needs. The caterpillars are earthbound eating machines, sometimes grotesquely ornamented with colors and spikes and camouflage patterns quite unlike the adult butterfly's coloration. The adults are ethereally airborne for their essential function of reproduction, though many butterflies sip nectar as food and in so doing serve a secondary function, ranking second only to bees as beneficial pollinators of fruits and other crops. Other lepidopterans are unable to eat and live only long enough to fulfill their reproductive role.

Some adult moths have hearing so sensitive they can detect the echolocating signals of Lepidoptera-eating bats. When they pick up a bat's ultrasonic signals night-flying moths immediately respond by making evasive maneuvers. Lepidopteran eyes are capable of detecting ultraviolet light, by which they can identify flower patterns invisible to less sophisticated eyes.

As impressive in its own way as anything else about the members of the order Lepidoptera is an extraordinarily keen sense of smell. The olfactory organs of butterflies and moths are located chiefly on their antennae. Since smell is the key factor in enabling a male to locate a prospective mate, the matter is critical to survival of the species. The female aroma has been detected by male moths as far as a mile away. The record, however, is held by a Chinese silkworm moth, which is capable of picking up the alluring scent of a female nearly seven miles distant.

Wing scales of a cecropia moth

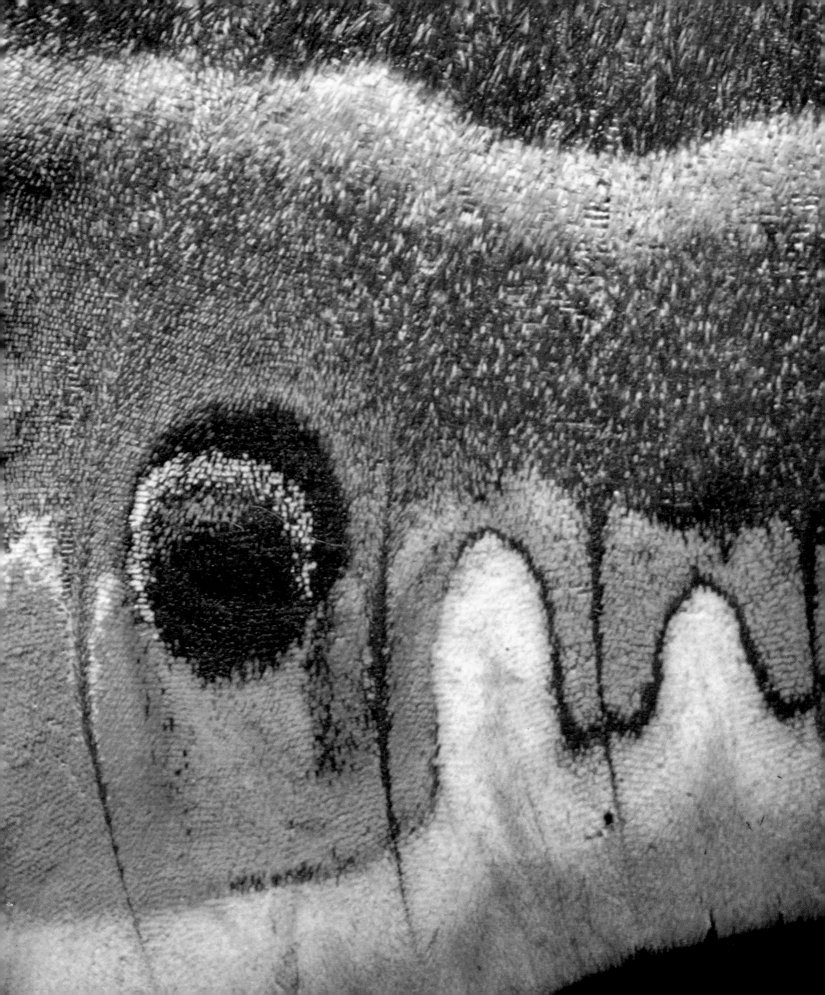

The Drama of Metamorphosis

The transmutation of a crawling larval caterpillar into a magnificent, flame-colored monarch butterfly is one of nature's more spectacular marvels. Metamorphosis begins at the moment the larva emerges from the egg and continues through five molts from the larval to the pupal stage. The caterpillar munches leaves constantly to nourish the incipient adult within its brightly colored skin.

Its diet is milkweed, a plant that is poisonous to most animals but not to monarch caterpillars. Such immunity provides a lifelong protection from predators, which recognize these milkweed carriers by their so-called "warning coloration" and carefully avoid both the caterpillar and the adult monarch after it emerges from the pupal stage in all its flamboyant glory.

Hatching from the delicately fluted egg its mother has attached to a leaf, a monarch larva offers no clue to the gorgeous creature it will eventually become.

A caterpillar that is ready to pupate attaches itself to a leaf with a patch of silk. Its skin splits, revealing the pupa.

Development of the mature insect begins inside a pupa by literally recycling the tissues of the caterpillar.

A gold-studded chrysalis shelters the pupating butterfly. Most monarch butterflies pupate for two to three weeks.

106

An infant caterpillar quickly darkening in color gets down to the first order of business: eating its rubbery eggshell. Already the larva has 16 legs, including six that will eventually become its adult limbs.

At the fifth molt, a caterpillar already flaunts the characteristic warning colors that proclaim to would-be predators that it is a distasteful—even poisonous—carrier of milkweed.

In the final, most dramatic stage of metamorphosis, a young butterfly pushes its swelling thorax through its shell.

A young monarch grasps its shell, pulls free and begins "pumping up"—forcing blood into its hollow wings.

With its sensitive tongue already rolled, the young butterfly rests while its wings harden in preparation for flight.

Monarchical Migration

Every autumn the monarch butterflies of North America take off in an annual southward hegira that would put many migratory birds to shame. The millions of frail-looking creatures come from as far away as southern Canada and fly as many as 2,000 miles. Monarchs that live west of the continental divide fly to the California coast; the easterners journey via Florida and the Gulf Coast and settle high in the Mexican *altiplano* northwest of Mexico City.

The wayfarers invariably follow the same routes year after year, stopping along the way to feed on myriad wildflowers; goldenrod (below) is a particular favorite. Once at their winter headquarters, they flock together on trees in dense, fluttering masses (opposite), though they usually arrive in groups of a dozen or less. In the spring the monarchs fly north again. Along the way, the females deposit their fertilized eggs on milkweed plants. By the time the round trip is finished, virtually all of the original southbound migrants are dead.

The Masqueraders

It is sundown in an autumn woodland. A bit of bird excrement suddenly comes to life and waddles off on little caterpillar feet in search of food. A flake of lichen detaches itself from a tree trunk and flutters away on moth wings. Three Kallima butterflies alight on a low bush, close their bright hind wings exposing the drab under surface (left) and freeze into an uncanny imitation of dry leaves.

The remarkable disguises of butterflies, moths and their caterpillars have taken three forms: 1) protective resemblance, assuming the shape of something else, like a moth that poses as a thorn (above); 2) mimicry, imitating dangerous or poisonous creatures that are shunned by predators; and 3) crypsis, or camouflage, melting into a natural background such as moss, leaves or lichens.

Such masquerades are not conscious or deliberate changes wrought by the insects; they are the result of natural selection. When a mutant butterfly happens by chance to take on protective coloring or form and survives, while its undisguised brethren perish, the changes are passed on to some of its offspring, and after many generations become characteristic of the species—a masquerade that is a striking example of survival of the fittest.

The dangerous-looking creature at left is not a wasp at all; it has no sting and might provide a succulent morsel if the birds of its native Jamaica were aware that it is actually a harmless moth, species Sesiidae, one of the insect kingdom's grand masters of mimicry. A remarkable example of protective resemblance is displayed by the lower twig in the picture at left, below. When it moves, the "twig" is easily identifiable as an inchworm or measuring worm of the family Geometridae. The windblown "seed" at right, below, is actually a cryptic caterpillar, disdained by hoodwinked predators that would gobble it up if they realized its true identity.

111

Togetherness

Symbiosis, a common natural arrangement under which two dissimilar organisms live together for mutual benefit, is nowhere more vividly illustrated than in the relationship between butterflies or moths and flowers. In the simplest symbiotic scenario, a butterfly burrows into a blossom to get at its nectar and at the same time fertilizes the bloom with pollen from the last flower it visited.

In a refinement of the process, specialized equipment, such as the unusually developed mouth parts of some moths that can probe deeply into blossoms' nectar reservoirs, evolved as flower and insect grew more complex and symbiotically dependent on each other. An example of the ultimate symbiotic union—called obligatory mutualism —involves an inextricable interdependency between the yucca moth and the creamy-white yucca flower (opposite). The moth must lay its eggs in the ovaries of the plant and is in turn the only insect agent that will cross-pollinate the yucca flowers. Without each other neither moth nor plant could survive.

In a demonstration of simple symbiosis, a rose-colored primrose moth nuzzles deep into a flower (above) to get at the nectar. In the process it gets a thorough dusting of pollen on its scaly wings and body, which will fertilize the next flower it visits.

A more sophisticated symbiotic act is performed at right by a European hummingbird hawk moth. Like other members of the hawk moth family, it has evolved an extraordinarily long sucking proboscis—half again the length of its body—and is one of the few insects able to reach the deepest nectar glands of a flower.

Wait Till Next Year

One of the most curious symbiotic relationships in the insect world occurs between the lustrous imperial blue butterfly of Australia, *Jalmenus evagoras*, and an unimpressive-looking black ant of the genus Iridomyrmex. Imperial blue females invariably lay their eggs in the branches of a wattle tree (left). When the caterpillars appear, they are immediately taken into custody by swarms of ants that guard them from parasites and predators.

As if exacting payment for this protection, the ants "milk" the caterpillars for a fluid that they secrete. When the larvae enter the pupal stage, they no longer produce this attractive substance; but the ants continue to stand guard over them, even though they no longer receive any fluid. When the mature butterflies emerge from their chrysalids, a strange change occurs, and the erstwhile protectors turn on the fledglings and attack them, apparently under the impression that they are menacing the pupae. After the last butterflies have fled for their lives, the ants go underground and await another symbiotic summer and another generation of caterpillars to watch over.

A brand-new caterpillar wanders over a clutch of its unhatched brethren (above). Soon, a phalanx of ant guards will arrive. Claiming its reward, an ant strokes the seventh dorsal segment of a caterpillar (right) until it emits a droplet from a "honey gland."

Ants stand guard over a pair of pupae in the fork of a wattle tree, an acacia common to southeastern Australia. Inexplicably, female imperial blue butterflies lay their eggs only in specific individual trees, returning to the same trees they hatched on generation after generation and avoiding nearby wattles in the same stand of trees.

A newly emerged imperial blue poises momentarily while its wings inflate before taking flight. Unlike most butterflies, the blues must literally burst from their chrysalids and take to the air in a matter of seconds to escape the once benevolent ants, now their enemies, which would otherwise kill them. Their iridescent blue upper wings can be seen only when the butterflies are in flight.

Marked for Survival

Their exquisite colors and ethereal grace have marked butterflies as the inspiration of poets, the symbol of immortal life and the most popular of all insects. Those exotic colors and wing patterns, though, are not just whimsical accidents on the environmental palette. They serve very definite purposes.

Some markings, like the six staring eyes on the wings of the American buckeye (top row, center), may be bluffs, serving to scare off enemies; the eye on the wood nymph wing (bottom row, far right) is a target spot, which can draw a predator's eye away from vital organs in the body to the less vulnerable wing. Other color patterns, despite their conspicuous elegance, are marvelous camouflage in the flowery haunts of their owners: the painted lady (top row, far right), most widely distributed of all butterflies, and the tiger swallowtail (bottom row, left), called the "flying flower."

American copper

Western tiger swallowtail

Parnalius polyxena

Buckeye

American painted lady

Eastern tailed blue

Wood nymph

117

Cinderella Stories

In the world of Lepidoptera, coming events do not cast their shadows before them. As the pictures on these pages show, any resemblance between a lumpish caterpillar and the dazzling adult in its future is impossible to detect. The prickly-looking, polka-dotted larva directly below gives no hint of the elegantly striped zebra butterfly it is destined to become when it reaches maturity.

And no one would suspect that the green caterpillar with the comically fierce face would turn into a spicebush swallowtail, one of the loveliest butterflies in a family of beauties (bottom row, left). The concertina caterpillar in the top row at right eventually becomes a gorgeous moth, named after Polyphemus, the one-eyed giant of Greek mythology, even though its wings display four fake eyes. The larva of the satiny regal, or royal walnut moth, (opposite, center) is so hideous that it has a fierce common name of its own—hickory horned devil—despite its total harmlessness. And the imperial moth (bottom row, opposite) apparently did not lose the art of camouflage in its transition from a gaudy green caterpillar.

Zebra caterpillar

Zebra butterfly

Spicebush swallowtail caterpillar

Spicebush swallowtail adult

Polyphemus caterpillar

Polyphemus moth

Hickory horned devil

Royal walnut moth

Imperial caterpillar

Imperial moth

Pas de Deux

When they mate, moths execute a kind of fluttering aerial ballet that culminates in a graceful coupling, like that of the eyed hawk moths at left. The male moth grasps a twig or other support with his forelegs and, aided by powerful chitinous claspers at the tip of his abdomen, grips his dangling partner firmly.

Unlike the diurnal butterflies, which can recognize their own kind in daylight even though their eyes are weak, many moths are nocturnal and must rely almost entirely on their remarkable sense of smell in order to pursue the mating game. Female moths exude a heady perfume, which males can detect with a keen olfactory apparatus in their antennae and follow to its source, often in total darkness or over long distances. Some male moths have dense feathery antennae; these are likely to have a sharper sense of smell than their less well-endowed brethren. Females use their sense of smell only to detect food plants and suitable places to lay their eggs (below). As a consequence, their olfactory sense and their antennae are not nearly so well developed as those of male moths.

In a controlled laboratory situation, a female polyphemus moth deposits a dozen lozengelike eggs on a rotten stump. In the wild, polyphemus moths never lay all their eggs in a single location; instead, they scatter them two or three at a time in several sites so that if one batch should be destroyed, others will survive. When laying her eggs, the female uses an organ called an ovipositor, which can be extended or retracted like a telescope to fasten each egg firmly in place.

The Beauty Part

When it comes to looks, moths are a mixed lot. Some are ugly, drab and tattered specimens that only a moth could love; others are among the most dazzling beauties of the animal kingdom. The spectacular quartet depicted here is living proof that, in moths at least, size has nothing to do with beauty. The two handsome examples at the top of these pages are among the largest of all moths, and two of the tiniest, greatly magnified, are shown below.

The largest moth in eastern North America, the boldly marked cecropia moth (right), has a wing-span of five inches and is easily identified by the characteristic crescents on its wings. Its comparably large southern European cousin, the Spanish moon moth (opposite, top), with its exquisite pastel coloring and feathered antennae, suggests a Broadway showgirl. In the larval stage, both moths spin silk, although their product has no commercial value.

The tiny white plume moth (below) is a member of the microlepidoptera group, which makes up in numbers— 25,000 members—what it lacks in size. On the wing, the white plume is the fan dancer of moths. In repose it furls its wings tightly so that it looks like nothing more than a twig.

Not to be confused with its cousin, the equally beauteous luna moth, the Spanish moon (right) is a night-flying inhabitant of mountain pine forests. The minuscule fairy moth (below) is a voracious destroyer of plants and shrubs in its California habitat. Outsized antennae, which mark the male of the species, are believed to aid in aerial maneuvering required to find a mate.

123

Butterflies of several different species gather together to feast on wildflowers in an Arkansas Meadow.

Credits

Cover—J. Robinson, Photo Researchers, Inc. 1—A. Blank, Bruce Coleman, Inc. 5—J. Lurie, B.C. 6–7—S. Dalton, P.R. 9—Co Rentmeester. 15—M. Fogden, B.C. 16–17—S. Krasemann, P.R. 17—J. Shaw, B.C. 18–19—R. Head, P.R. 19—J. Shaw, B.C. 20 (left)—Oxford Scientific Films, (right)—M. Fogden, B.C. 21—Oxford Scientific Films. 22—S. Krasemann, Nat'l. Audubon Society, P.R. 23—P. Ward, B.C. 24—W. Bayer, B.C. 25—H. Rogers, P.R. 26 (left)—Dr. J. Cooke, Oxford Scientific Films, (right)—M. Fogden, B.C. 27 (left)—Jen & Des Bartlett, B.C., (right)—Oxford Scientific Films, B.C. 28 (left)—J. Carmichael, P.R., (right)—E. Degginger, B.C. 29—R.E. Pelham, B.C. 30—E.R. Degginger, B.C. 31 (top and bottom)—Dr. J. Cooke, Oxford Scientific Films. 32—G. Dodge & D.R. Thompson, B.C. 33—T. McHugh, P.R. 34 (left)—T. McHugh, Steinhart Aquarium, P.R., (right)—Z. Leszczynski, Animals Animals. 35—Z. Leszczynski, Animals Animals. 40–41—W. B. Allen, Jr., Nat'l. Audubon Society Collection, P.R. 43—S. Dalton, P.R. 44 (top)—C. Latch, B.C., (bottom)—D. Overcash, B.C. 45—R. Kinne, P.R. 46–47—Dr. J. Cooke, B.C. 49—S. Bisserot, B.C. 50—P. Ward, B.C. 51—L. Quitt, P.R. 52—A. Eisenstaedt, Time Inc. 53 (top)—G. Dodge & D. Thompson, B.C., (bottom)—H. Uible, P.R. 54—J. Flannery, B.C. 55—M. Holmes, Animals Animals. 59—S. Dalton, P.R. 60 (left)—H. Groskinsky, Time Inc., (right)—A. Kalnik, P.R. 61 (top, left)—Oxford Scientific Films, (top, right)—L.L. Rue III, P.R., (bottom, left)—J. Carmichael, Jr., P.R. (bottom, right)—R. Hermes, P.R. 63—Dr. J. Cooke, Oxford Scientific Films. 64 (top, left)—Oxford Scientific Films, B.C., (top, right)—H. Darrow, B.C., (center)—L. Quitt, P.R., (bottom, right)—J. Robinson, P.R. 65 (top, left)—S. Dalton, P.R., (top, right)—Oxford Scientific Films, (center, left)—S. Dalton, P.R., (center, right)—P. Ward, B.C., (bottom, left)—K. Brate, P.R., (bottom, right)—B. Campbell, B.C. 66–67, 67—Oxford Scientific Films. 69—H. Reinhard, B.C. 70–71—P. Ward, B.C. 72—R. Carr, B.C. 73 (top, left)—Dr. J. Cooke, B.C., (top, right)—R. Carr, B.C., (bottom, left)—H. Darrow, B.C., (bottom, right)—K. Brate, P.R. 74—L.L. Rue III, P.R. 76 (left)—R. Mendez, Animals Animals, (right)—H. Rogers, P.R. 77 (left)—B.C. (right)—R. Parker, P.R. 79—S. Dalton, P.R. 80—Oxford Scientific Films, B.C., 81—S. Dalton, P.R. 82—Oxford Scientific Films, B.C., 83 (top)—S. Dalton, P.R., (bottom)—Oxford Scientific Films, B.C. 84 (top)—Oxford Scientific Films, B.C., (bottom)—T. Davidson, Nat'l. Audubon Society Collection, P.R. 85, 86—S. Dalton, P.R. 87 (left)—E. Degginger, B.C., (right)—R. Mendez, Animals Animals. 88—A. Blank, B.C. 89 (top)—J. Clawson, P.R., (bottom)—E. Degginger, B.C. 90–91—R. Hermes, Nat'l. Audubon Society, P.R. 91—E. Degginger, B.C. 92–95—C. Bavignoli, Time Inc. 94—M. Havelin, P.R. 95—M. Fogden, B.C. 105—W. Greenwood, B.C. 106 (top)—Oxford Scientific Films, B.C., (bottom, left)—D. Overcash, B.C., (bottom, center); (bottom, right)—E. Degginger, B.C. 107 (top, left); (top, right)—D. Overcash, B.C., (bottom, left); (bottom, center); (bottom, right)—E. Degginger, B.C. 108—D. Overcash, B.C. 109—G. Lepp, B.C. 110 (top)—M. Fogden, B.C., (bottom)—A. Blank, B.C. 111 (top)—J. Carmichael, B.C., (bottom, left)—J. Robinson, P.R., (bottom, right)—Oxford Scientific Films, B.C. 112 (top)—V. Weinland, Nat'l. Audubon Society, P.R., (bottom)—H. Eisenbeiss, P.R. 113—M. Fogden, B.C. 114–115—Oxford Scientific Films. 116 (top); (bottom, left)—J. Shaw, B.C., (bottom, right)—T. Angermayer, P.R. 117 (top, left); (top, right)—D. Overcash, B.C., (bottom, left)—L. West, B.C., (bottom, right)—R. Mendez, Animals Animals. 118 (top, left); (top, right)—E. Degginger, B.C., (bottom, left)—R. Simons, P.R., (bottom, right)—E. Degginger, B.C. 119 (top, left)—J. Robinson, P.R., (top, right)—S. McKeever, P.R., (center, left)—J. Robinson, P.R., (center, right)—K. Maslowski, P.R., (bottom, left)—S. McKeever, P.R., (bottom, right)—J. Carmichael, Jr., B.C. 120—T. Angermayer, P.R. 121—E. Degginger, B.C. 122 (top)—L. Stone, P.R., (bottom)—N. Fox-Davies, B.C. 123 (top)—S. Bisserot, B.C., (bottom)—D. Rentz, B.C. 124–125—T. Daniel, B.C. 128—A. Blank, B.C.

Photographs on endpapers are used courtesy of Time-Life Picture Agency, Russ Kinne and Stephen Dalton of Photo Researchers, Inc., and Nina Leen.

Film sequence on page 8 is from "The Spider," a program in the Time-Life Television series *Wild, Wild World of Animals*.

ILLUSTRATION on page 10–11 by Lorelle Raboni. Paintings on page 12, by Alice Gray, courtesy of the American Museum of Natural History. Illustrations on page 13 by Enid Kotschnig. Those on pages 36–38 by André Durenceau, those on pages 56–57 by George Herriman, those on pages 96–97 by John Groth.

Bibliography

NOTE: Asterisk at the left means that a paperback volume is also listed in *Books in Print*.

Borror, Donald J., and Delong, Dwight M., *An Introduction to the Study of Insects*. Doubleday, 1959.

*Buchsbaum, Ralph, *Animals Without Backbones*. University of Chicago Press, 1962.

Comstock, John, *The Spider Book*. Doubleday, Doran, 1940.

Crompton, John, *The Life of the Spider*. Houghton Mifflin, 1951.

Eisner T., and Eisner H. E., "Mystery of a Millipede." *Natural History Magazine*. Vol. LXXIV, No. 3 (March 1965) pp. 30–37.

Essig, E. O., *Insects of Western North America*. The Macmillan Company, 1926.

Gaul, Albro T., *The Wonderful World of Insects*. Rinehart, 1953.

*Goetsch, Wilhelm, *Insects*. University of Michigan Press, 1957.

Grzimek, Bernhard, *Animal Life Encyclopedia*, Vols. 1 and 2. Van Nostrand Reinhold, 1975.

*Evans, Howard Ensign, *Wasp Farm*. The Natural History Press, 1963.

Farb, Peter, *The Insects*. Time-Life, 1962.

Haskins, Caryl P., *Of Ants and Men*. Norwood Editions, 1945.

Hutchins, Ross E., *Insects*. Prentice-Hall, 1966.

Klots, Alexander, *1001 Questions Answered About Insects*. Dodd, Mead, 1961.

——— and Klots, Elsie, *Living Insects of the World*. Doubleday, 1959.

Larousse Encyclopedia of the Animal World. Larousse, 1975.

Linsenmaier, Walter, *Insects of the World*. McGraw-Hill, 1972.

Macy, Ralph W., and Shepard, Harold H., *Butterflies*. University of Minnesota Press, 1941.

Michener, Charles D., *The Social Behavior of Bees*. Harvard University Press, 1974.

Pain, Nesta, *Grassblade Jungle*. Coward-McCann, 1959.

Richards, O. W., *The Social Insects*. Harper & Row, 1953.

Ross, Herbert H., *A Textbook of Entomology*. John Wiley, 1965.

Rowland-Entwistle, Theodore, and Oxford Scientific Films Ltd., *The World You Never See: Insect Life*. Hamlyn, 1976.

Savory, Theodore H., *Introduction to Arachnology.* Frederick Muller, 1974.

Shuttlesworth, Dorothy, *The Story of Spiders.* Doubleday, 1959.

Sisson, Robert F., "The Spider That Lives Under Water." *National Geographic.* Vol. 141, No. 5 (May 1972), pp. 694–701.

Sudd, John H., *Introduction to the Behavior of Ants.* St. Martin, 1967.

*Teale, Edwin Way, *Near Horizons.* Pyramid Publications, 1967.

Urquhart, Fred A., "Found at Last: the Monarch's Winter Home." *National Geographic.* Vol. 150, No. 2 (August 1976) pp. 161–173.

*Von Frisch, Karl, *The Dancing Bees.* Harcourt, Brace and World, 1953.

Wilson, Edward O. *The Insect Societies.* Harvard University Press, 1971.

Zahl, Paul A., "What's So Special About Spiders?" *National Geographic.* Vol. 140, No. 2 (August 1971), pp. 190–219.

*Zim, Herbert S., and Cottam, Clarence, *Insects: A Guide to Familiar American Insects.* Western Publishing, 1951.

Index